CREATURES OF CONTACT

"I was introduced and trained in the Birkman Method when hired in human resources at Cox Enterprises. Cox has used the Birkman successfully since 1989 to build better self-awareness in our employees and to improve and enhance how teams work together. It has become a key component of my HR practice, and I can remember attending my first Birkman conference where I met Dr. Birkman and Sharon Birkman Fink, the author. I felt such warmth and, dare I say, an authentic connection in those moments. At Cox we have used the Birkman to connect people through similarities and differences. So I think that it is wonderful and appropriate that Sharon write this book, especially at this particular time in our world. It's a great read, and I highly recommend it."

Ursula Brown McCandless
Senior Manager, Org and Talent Development
Cox Enterprises, Atlanta

"Historically the gold standard of personality assessments in leadership coaching, team building, and career exploration, the Birkman Method is now at the forefront of capitalizing on new technologically advanced digital methodologies and emerging discoveries in neuroplasticity. In this book, Sharon Birkman presents compelling arguments that the Birkman—based on data statistically validated by millions of individuals across the globe—can be used to help bridge the distance between possible feelings of isolation and loneliness in order to reduce misunderstanding among diverse generations, genders, and cultures."

Susan Diamond
Vice President of Chapter Chairs and Chief Learning Officer
Women Presidents' Organization

"Sharon Birkman's *Creatures of Contact* explores and provides guidance around a core tenant of human experience: we need each other to find joy and fulfillment. Her deep knowledge of the Birkman Method provides an important vocabulary that allows us to reeducate ourselves in the art of interpersonal relationships. It would be hard to quantify the benefits personally, professionally, and organizationally for individuals who take Sharon's insights to heart. I fully recommend *Creatures of Contact* to those seeking ways to deepen their capacity to meaningfully connect."

Matthew Gosney, EdD
Vice President, Organizational Development
Human Resource Services
UC Health

"Sharon Birkman's book is fundamentally about kindness, vulnerability, and courage and why it is essential for leaders to find ways to enhance their purpose by learning the needs of those in their span of care. We are continuously seeking personal and professional growth by straddling the line between powerful technology and what Sharon calls 'meaningful human connection.' I've been using the Birkman assessment since 2005, in both business and academia, and have coached hundreds of executives who are transformed through understanding themselves and others using the Birkman Method. This book is a must for people at all levels in their careers who are seeking to become transformational leaders."

Dr. Cynthia McCloud
Director, Food Industry Programs, Executive Education
Adjunct Professor, Marshall School of Business
USC Marshall School of Business

"Educators, leaders, and trainers have always known that the Birkman Method was not just a personality assessment but a tool that reflects the true complexity of people's behaviors, expectations, and mindset. Because of this, it is the best resource available to help people honestly assess how they can better connect and work with others around them. *Creatures of Contact* looks at how we, as complex individuals living in a fractured and lonely world, can more meaningfully communicate and connect with one another."

Jamie Belinne
Assistant Dean
Rockwell Career Center
C.T. Bauer College of Business
University of Houston

"In any organization, the culture is and should be about the people. And with this, the human connection is essential. To know and better understand how everyone shows up on the outside and how they act under stress as well as their needs to be more productive and fulfilled, the Birkman Method is the only tool in which to assess these specific traits. Limb UNLimited is utilizing this important assessment for our clients to support superiors and create a stronger culture for a more successful outcome."

Biddie Webb
Partner
Limb Design

"In a world increasingly driven by big data and analytics the desire of many organizations is to reduce people down to a formula. But people are human and they want connection. And with that connection their ability to achieve in communities and teams far exceeds anything that can be predicted by numbers in a test. The Birkman Method keeps the 'personality' test very human. It reflects the complexity in us all. Its ability to help us understand our motivations in the context of others helps us to be better teammates, friends, parents, and neighbors. A timely work as loneliness, anxiety, and depression continue to increase as many look for counterfeits for connection with others."

Mark Harrell
Autodesk

"In a pivotal time in human history where the need for relationship is greater than ever, this brilliant and insightful book shines a bright, hopeful light on the importance and power of human connection. With our ever-increasing reliance on technology and social media, this book is filled with wisdom, understanding, and experience about the importance of meaningful contact in our personal and professional lives and what we must do to ensure our social connections. Building upon decades of research and experience through the lens of social psychology and the power of the Birkman Method, Sharon Birkman offers a framework to truly understand the needs of another person along with a vision and perspective about the importance of deep connections and a challenge to steward them well. This book is an important, powerful, and timely gift, offering hope and promise for our generation and generations to come."

Dana W. Scannell, PhD
Organizational Psychologist and President
Scannell & Wight

"As a Birkman professional in Korea, time to time I've been asked if the western assessment applies in an Asian community. Surprisingly, the answer is definitely yes. And once they've experienced this powerful tool, there's no need to explain further. That's why the Birkman Method is so successful and has grown so fast in Korea. Because no matter what gender, nationality, age, or even culture, we are just human who all need healthy relationships in this lonely planet, knowing themselves and knowing others. *Creatures of Contact* is based on the story of Sharon Birkman, who deeply understands what it means to be human. That is one more reason I should admire her along with her great leadership and special, sincere heart."

Elly Hwang
Birkman Korea Team Manager

"Self-awareness and awareness of others are two of the most important skills we can demonstrate when we are connecting with people. Whether coaching an executive leader, constructing project teams, career coaching, or sharing with couples who want to have stronger relationships, I have found that the Birkman Method provides powerful insights into how we work better with others. Captured in a way that only Sharon Birkman can do, *Creatures of Contact: Why You Need More than a Personality Test* helps us understand how to collaborate at our best!"

Wanda J. Hayes, PhD
Senior Director, Learning & Organizational Development
Emory University

What can we learn from their watery ends?

Is there some lesson on how to be friends?

I think what it means is that central to living

a life that is good

is a life that's forgiving.

We're creatures of contact,

regardless of whether we kiss

or we wound.

Still, we must come together.

Though it may spell destruction,

we still ask for more—

since it beats staying dry

but so lonely on shore.

So we make ourselves open

while knowing full well

it's essentially saying,

please, come pierce my shell.

—David Rakoff,
"Speak Now or Forever Hold Your Peace"

SHARON BIRKMAN

CREATURES

WHY YOU NEED
MORE THAN A
PERSONALITY TEST

OF CONTACT

ForbesBooks

Published by ForbesBooks, Charleston, South Carolina.
Member of Advantage Media Group.

ForbesBooks is a registered trademark, and the ForbesBooks colophon is a trademark of Forbes Media, LLC.

Printed in the United States of America.

10 9 8 7 6 5 4 3 2 1

ISBN: 978-1-94663-344-6
LCCN: 2019919283

Cover design by Melanie Cloth.
Layout design by Wesley Strickland.

This publication is designed to provide accurate and authoritative information in regard to the subject matter covered. It is sold with the understanding that the publisher is not engaged in rendering legal, accounting, or other professional services. If legal advice or other expert assistance is required, the services of a competent professional person should be sought.

 Advantage Media Group is proud to be a part of the Tree Neutral® program. Tree Neutral offsets the number of trees consumed in the production and printing of this book by taking proactive steps such as planting trees in direct proportion to the number of trees used to print books. To learn more about Tree Neutral, please visit **www.treeneutral.com**.

Since 1917, the Forbes mission has remained constant. Global Champions of Entrepreneurial Capitalism. ForbesBooks exists to further that aim by bringing the Stories, Passion, and Knowledge of top thought leaders to the forefront. ForbesBooks brings you The Best in Business. To be considered for publication, please visit **www.forbesbooks.com**.

July 18, '24

This book is gratefully dedicated to the people lovers who have walked with us over the years, using the social science of Birkman to deepen understanding and bring people together.

Brian,
    Welcome to our
Birkman family!
        With warmest
            wishes,
                Sharon

CONTENTS

NOTE TO READER

I f you've heard of *The Birkman Method*©, you might wonder at my subtitle. You may ask: "But isn't the Birkman just that—a personality test?"

It is, and more. From one simple assessment, we can learn about one another in multiple ways. We identify three positive dimensions that address perceptions, mindset, and motivations, making Birkman more than a personality test.

In fact, the Birkman is, first and foremost, a perceptual analysis that melds purpose, personality, and perceptions into one brief assessment. The distinctiveness of this approach rests on realizing the power of human perceptions: *How do I see you, how do I see myself, and what are the activities I most enjoy doing?*

Originally called "A Test of Social Comprehension," the Birkman is a test only in the sense of being a metric, or a way to objectively assess. Not a test to pass or fail but a way to better understand yourself and the world you share with others. Recalling that the word *comprehend* is a synonym for *understanding*, this makes sense.

These are my professional reasons for the subtitle. There's another reason, one that is personal.

I know the Birkman to be a premier psychological instrument for leaders and teams, coaching and careers, but at the end of the day, it is still only an assessment. I worry that in our increasingly digitized world, people often feel more disconnected than ever. In so many ways, we continue to battle chronic loneliness. I believe it's always been there, but I am convinced we share a desperate need to discover ways to see (perceive) each other in more understanding ways. As powerful, flawed, talented, and vulnerable *human* beings, we've never stopped needing one another to survive. Today's technology continues to expand our horizons, but no virtual reality has yet managed to replace a warm and appreciative conversation, and the best digital image is still no substitute for a warm hug or a smile.

To the core, we humans remain social creatures, born to crave human contact and designed for connection that's not limited to a device or a screen. For our Birkman Method to come alive and rise to its highest levels, some caring *human contact* remains a valuable part of the equation. When the Birkman Method with its social science is combined with a knowledgeable person who is willing to listen and engage in compassionate dialogue—an irreplaceable alchemy may occur. For these reasons, Rakoff is right. We are indeed creatures of contact, and we do need more than a personality test. We need one another.

CHAPTER 1

SPEAK NOW

The meeting of two personalities is like the contact of two chemical reactions. If there is any reaction, both are transformed.

—Dr. Carl Jung

I t was Sunday, October 25, 2009. Driving to a family lunch, I was listening to NPR's *This American Life* when I heard David Rakoff read his poem "Speak Now or Forever Hold Your Peace." At the time, the United States had begun to reel from the Wall Street meltdown, and I was contemplating ideas for my first book, *The Birkman Method: Your Personality at Work*. I barely caught the end of Rakoff's version of the humorous, ironic fable, but the final lines of his poem, a rhyming retelling of Aesop's fable of the scorpion and the tortoise, struck me like a thunderbolt.

When I heard the poet say, "Central to living a life that is good is a life that's forgiving ... we're *creatures of contact*," I knew I had the title for the book I wanted to write. However difficult it is for us to get along, we're creatures who *need others* to survive. We seek ways to become our best selves, but ultimately, know we're incomplete without healthy relationships with one another. Since that moment, the truth of those words has never left me. In this way, I've been preparing for this book for nearly a decade, and it feels more relevant now than ever before.

At Birkman, we're in the business of social psychology. We provide the Birkman Method, a comprehensive assessment of interpersonal and occupational strengths. We work with organizations of all sizes to help them focus on the personal and professional development of their people. Throughout our history, the assessment that began on a small typewriter has managed to morph over its seven decades from one new technology to the next.

These days, technology itself is rapidly transforming how humans relate across the globe. Our digitally dominated world affects all our interactions: how we gather information and how we stay in touch. And while the digital revolution has changed our existence in many impressive ways for better and for worse, it's radically altered the ways we humans communicate and connect.

Despite the technology that enables more and more online connection, we can feel more disconnected than ever, and experts report that loneliness is on the rise. Chronic loneliness is seen among all ages and is quickly being viewed as an epidemic. Once heavily focused on the elderly, more and more studies reveal that our young people are facing new levels of loneliness. In fact, after a twelve-month investigation into the growing number of lonely individuals in the United Kingdom, in 2017 the British government deemed loneliness "a real and diagnosable scourge," worse for health than smoking multiple packs of cigarettes per day. Britain therefore appointed, for the first time, a Minister of Loneliness in 2018. With loneliness reaching new levels among a new generation of people, how do we curtail human disconnection in a technologically connected world? Because I've seen it work, I can tell you that one answer lies in the field of social psychology.

The psychology of emotional and social intelligence has come a long way since my dad first began his research on social comprehension in the late 1940s. My parents often said their original dream was to just "take Birkman to the world." This was an audacious goal for those early days when every report had to be hand scored, individually dictated, typed on a typewriter, and snail-mailed, but I admire their entrepreneurial optimism and have committed my own professional life to seeing it continue.

Today, Birkman is a global company with a presence on six continents. On a professional level, our assessment continues to empower individuals and companies with social science: leadership development, executive coaching, team building, talent selection, career transition, employee engagement, mergers, and negotiations. We work directly with people who work with other people to empower their relationships and performance. On a personal level, we've helped individuals find their careers, voices, confidence, and relevance amid the families and groups that surround them. It is hard for me to cite a sweeter moment than when someone tells me how their Birkman report improved their life. More than once, we've heard from a

Roger and Sue, 1945

Roger and Sue, 1995

manager or a spouse who handed someone their own Birkman report, saying, "Please read this. It's my owner's manual."

So perhaps my parents' dream was not so audacious after all. They'd be overjoyed to see how Birkman continues to reassure individuals, help teams, guide careers, and improve relationships wherever people live and work together.

Not long ago, we were expanding and updating our office space. As part of the reconfiguration, I was sorting through boxes of my father's old files. I came across an article he'd saved that expressed concern about the "current young people." According to this article, they're less loyal, more self-concerned, not motivated to work too hard, and overly focused on their own welfare and comfort. Because I'd been fielding questions about Millennials and Gen Z (namely, how were they showing up in our Birkman data?), I'd been hearing similar criticisms of today's young people, so this was an interesting find. Then I noticed the date on the article: it was 1997, referencing Gen X.

IF WE DRILL DOWN TO THE DEEPER LEVELS OF HUMAN PERCEPTIONS, BEHAVIORS, AND RELATIONSHIPS, HISTORY SOUNDS REMARKABLY FAMILIAR.

Perhaps it's a human thing: each generation tending to view their younger counterparts in a similar way. For me, it reinforced once again what Birkman data has shown us over the decades—that so many aspects of the human condition seem to remain consistent over time. We appear to change outwardly in so many ways, but apparently, we do not change dramatically at the core levels of what makes us human. From generation to generation and from industry to industry, if we drill down to the deeper levels of human perceptions, behaviors, and relationships, history sounds remarkably familiar.

It's my position that history and perceptions repeat themselves because they are linked to our core humanity: the parts of us that are time transcending and universal. How do we face this challenge? How do we learn to value our own unique selves, gain a deeper understanding and acceptance of others, and live lives that are forgiving—of ourselves and of one another?

These are the questions that fascinated my psychologist father. And his dedication to understanding the powers of divergent perceptions and what motivated people's behavior formed the backdrop of my childhood.

In every way, those early years were an uphill battle for my parents. In the 1960s, choosing to place his social psychology on a huge IBM mainframe, my dad became an early adopter of computer technology. He realized early on the value of keeping his data for research. The millions of questionnaires we've processed since then from around the world confirm the natural complexity of human behaviors and yield valuable insights into social comprehension—understanding people and the power of their perceptions. This is the reason we're still here and is the backbone of all we do at Birkman International.

These days, as technology propels psychology and neuroscience to new levels of understanding, personality tests are abundant and can easily be dismissed as an all-too-familiar concept. With so many options on the market, people can feel they are "assessed to death." And while many of these tests can be fun as icebreakers or team activities, their value may be limited when it comes to true professional development and transformational growth.

Human personality, as you've probably noticed, is vastly complex. To ease understanding, it helps to assign a symbol or a label to describe the parts of ourselves we call our "personality," and these symbols can offer a convenient way to simplify our natural complexity. There is nothing wrong with this, provided it doesn't stop there. None of us are one-dimensional, and we never want anyone to feel we've confined them to a label or defined them with a single category. Because Birkman differs from all other personality tests, I'm grateful for these pages.

This book is not a memoir or an academic explanation but a message from my heart that I've carried for over a decade. I've been privileged to carry my father's legacy for seventeen years, and this is the book I've wanted to write since Rakoff's words struck me so deeply. We've always known our social science has the power to affirm and motivate people. What if it could also be used to create healthier relationships and even a more deeply connected global culture?

The world has known strife and division since recorded history began, but speaking as a citizen of the United States, we seem to have become more dangerously divided today than ever before in my lifetime. These pages will describe how social psychology and the work my father began all those years ago holds one key to a way our divisions might start to heal, a way to break out of our prisons of *misperceptions* and misunderstanding to come closer together in our day-to-day relationships, a way to be freer of judgment and defensiveness.

As mentioned, many people will naturally refer to the Birkman Method as a personality test, and they're not wrong. But Birkman reaches further to include *motivations, perceptions, interests, and mindset* in addition to what we call "personality." This multifaceted view affords several nuanced and layered dimensions for better understanding of self and others.

As a perceptual analysis, the distinct power of the Birkman resides in identifying how we see ourselves *combined with* what we expect of others in the world around us. As we will discuss in depth in the following pages, our perceptions are addressed in the social context of self and others. While we have, like most other assessments, relied on the use of some symbols and colors for convenience, we will never assess an individual's personality with a single label or dimension. To perceive means "to see," and we see people on multiple levels that include:

1. How we perceive ourselves along with what we expect from others in our world

2. The core interests that motivate us and keep us engaged

3. Ways to recognize when we're experiencing nonproductive stress

Birkman shows how we're each composed of a dynamic, kaleidoscopic combination of traits that are uniquely our own. These traits are both learned from our social environment and hardwired from our DNA, and they have some bandwidth to adapt and change depending on who we're with or what we're focused on doing. This is one reason people often feel their personality changes, or at least appears to change. We can, in fact, change—not the essence of who we're born to be—but we can *and do* change *how we relate* to others when our team or social environment changes. We can also change our behaviors when we feel we should adapt to a more socially desirable behavioral style, or an employee may appear to "change" when assigned to a different boss or a different team.

Recent neurological research is discovering more and more about the inherent neuroplasticity of the human brain. As humans, there's no denying we share a special capacity to adapt to other people and our social surroundings, and after all, this has been key to our very survival. Like the tiny shards of colored glass in a kaleidoscope, what we have in our perceptual kaleidoscope remains mostly consistent, but *how it looks* and plays out *can and will shift* from moment to moment, team to team, and relationship to relationship.

The research Birkman has compiled over the decades offers compelling insights into the human perceptions and kinds of behaviors that tend to remain stable over time. These are the relational perceptions we also share with our brothers and sisters around the globe. Understanding the similarities between generations, genders, and cultures can alter our worldview and improve our daily interactions with people around us, especially when we can begin to understand the more hidden and subtle nuances of our nature.

Because human behavior is endlessly complex, comprehending human perceptions is, and always will be, a challenge. As we'll discuss in the following chapters, when you see the power of your own perceptions and how this impacts your reality, it can empower you and your performance. Birkman data does this by showcasing your own unique combinations of interests, motivations, and strengths, enabling you to more fully affirm yourself and the people who share your world.

While I know Birkman as a premier assessment when it comes to teams, leadership, coaching, and career exploration, I also believe that in our superconnected digital world, we can often find ourselves feeling more isolated and fractured than ever. We're not data points or machines, and we need to see one another in more humane ways. However sophisticated our technology becomes, we remain living, breathing, powerful, flawed, and vulnerable human beings who've never stopped needing one another to prosper and flourish. As impressive as today's technology has become, it cannot replicate a friend's caring hug or a warm and welcoming smile.

Kai-Fu Lee, widely hailed as the oracle of artificial intelligence, was asked in an interview if AI, robots, and machine learning might eventually replace our need for other humans altogether. He replied, "I believe the AI revolution over the next few decades will be the most transformative change since the advent of electricity, but I don't think artificial general intelligence will ever entirely replace human connection." When asked why, Kai-Fu replied, "Because I believe in the sanctity of the soul."

Reflecting on his interview, I believe it is significant that he began his interview by sharing his own childhood story about a personal human connection. As a nine-year-old Chinese immigrant arriving at a school in Baltimore, he spoke little English and felt ostracized by his fourth-grade classmates. It was one very special teacher who turned this around for him. He remembers how this teacher saw his pain and, over the next months, volunteered to teach Kai-Fu English during his lunch breaks. Decades later, the man who's known for his expertise in AI chose to tell the story of how his connection with that one person who cared had forever transformed his life. Removing ourselves from quality human interaction is dangerous. Disconnecting from healthy human relationships hurts us on a personal level and diminishes our culture at large.[1]

At a time when so much of our daily life is online,
the need for meaningful person-to-person connection
and discussion may be even higher.

—Dr. Nitin Nohria, Dean of Harvard Business School

In another example of the positive impact of meaningful relationships, Dr. Robert Waldinger, a psychiatrist with Harvard Medical School, relates the findings of the longest research project ever conducted. Still ongoing, the study has spanned seventy-five

---

1   Kai-Fu Lee, "AI Superpowers: China, Silicon Valley and the New World," 2018. Interview with Scott Pelley.

years, from the early 1940s until the present; the researchers are now transitioning to the children of the original subjects. The goal of the Harvard project was to probe what ultimately makes people happiest and most secure over the span of their lifetime. The researchers chose 472 men to interview at the start and then continued to track and survey them annually throughout their life spans. They selected their Boston-area subjects, all white males, from two distinctly different categories: half were Ivy League (mainly Harvard) students, and the other half were young men from the poorest tenement neighborhoods of Boston.

Over the decades that followed, the research team continued to monitor them every year, and their overall conclusion was that the most significant impact on long-term happiness was not what one might readily assume. It was not wealth, fame, or career success. The most powerful predictor for their long-term happiness quotient was determined to be *meaningful human connection* with someone they trusted and could rely on to be there for them. It did not matter whether that person was a spouse, a friend, or a family member.

They also learned that these significant relationships did not have to be consistently smooth or always peaceful. In fact, they could and usually did include conflicts and disagreements, but in the final analysis, the subjects interviewed felt it was someone who had their back, a relationship they could count on to be there for them no matter what. Their research also reaffirmed that loneliness and isolation were not just problematic; they were, in fact, toxic killers, resulting in illness and shorter life spans. As the longest medical study ever conducted and continuing still, this Harvard Medical research concludes that the single most important predictor of overall happiness was the abiding presence in their lives of one or more healthy human relationships.

We are social creatures, born for human connection. For a Birkman report to truly come alive and rise to its best level, some human contact and caring connection is essential—whether it's with a coach, a supervisor, or the colleagues on your team. Armed with a more accurate understanding of yourself and those around you, you can become a stronger leader, a more effective coworker, and even a happier spouse or parent. The goal of this book is to highlight ways social relationships positively impact our well-being at every level, why self- and others-awareness is critical in maintaining healthy relationships, and how the Birkman Method can serve as a key to help you navigate many of the complexities of your human interactions.

> *Our most valuable currency is not money. Nor is it intelligence, attractiveness, fluency in 3-letter acronyms or the ability to write code or analyze a P&L statement. Our most valuable currency is relationships—the seed from which everything else grows, including success.*

—Susan Scott, author of ***Fierce Conversations***

TAKEAWAY TIPS

- Social isolation is toxic, even deadly, and there's widespread concern that loneliness is on the rise.

- Born into the world as interdependent social creatures, we're hardwired to crave positive, supportive human connection.

- Technology enables more ways to communicate, but no technology replicates or replaces the impact of healthy human relationships, the single biggest predictor of long-term happiness.

CHAPTER 2

STANDING ON OUR ROOTS

The meeting of eyes, the exchanging of words—
is to the psyche what oxygen is to the brain.

—Dr. Martha Beck

D espite being Texas born and raised, I never experienced horses until 2009, when I joined thirteen city slickers at an Arizona horse ranch for a three-day leadership course led by writer/coach Dr. Martha Beck. On the very first morning, overlooking a sawdust-encrusted arena, we watched as Koelle Simpson, Martha's horse-whispering cofacilitator, beckoned a horse to the center of the arena. Calm and confident, Koelle carried only a thin leather strap, which she tapped lightly on her thigh to signal the horse. We stared spellbound as the horse responded to her every silent gesture. When she tapped faster, the horse ran faster until she signaled it to reverse direction. A few moments later, she made another gesture, and the horse slowed to a trot. When she gave a final signal, the horse walked toward her, obe-diently following her from the arena. No words, no noise, no whips.

"Okay, your turn now," chirped Martha, explaining that now we'd each go down into the arena to interact with the horse as Koelle had demonstrated.

Seriously? I thought. *We just arrived! Don't we need more training?*

One by one, we entered the arena and proceeded to try, with "try" being the operative word. Owning my reluctant inner introvert, I managed to delay until, finally, everyone had tried to command the horse and I was last to go down. This meant I got to witness the variety of ways each person attempted to lead the horse and make it follow us. The more assertive types gave firm-sounding commands; others tried a softer approach, stroking the horse's mane, hoping to coax or cajole it into obedience. Neither approach worked. Not one of us was able to make the horse follow us as Koelle had done. Frus-trated and embarrassed, we returned to our seats, as clueless as the horse was confused.

Then Dr. Beck said, "Okay, friends, for the next fifteen minutes, I'm going to give you a brief lesson on understanding horses. First you need to know that horses are peaceful, nonpredatory vegetarians. Above all, they're social pack animals that prefer to travel in herds for safety. Their herds are *always* led by a mare. Her job is to guide the entire herd to a place where they can safely graze. If she is killed or disappears, regardless of the size of the herd, the other horses will instinctively know who the next lead mare should be.

"The stallions do not lead; they defend. Their job is to protect the herd, so they run alongside the herd and flank from the rear. This allows them to charge up as needed to save the herd from attacking predators. You need to know that horses are natural followers. They are authority-loving creatures who look to the lead mare for direction.

If you lead them properly, they will happily respond to your physical signals and emotional energies. I tell you all this because getting the horse to follow you is *not about you, it's about the horse*. It's about knowing what the *horse needs from you*, not what you need from the horse."

Armed now with this information, we each took our second turn in the arena. There was notable improvement. Once we'd learned something about the perceptions of the horse and what *its needs were*, our focus had shifted from what *we wanted the horse to do*, to *what the horse wanted and expected from us*.

This was a powerful moment for me because it exemplified one of the core truths I've learned from the Birkman: namely that it's less about me in building healthy relationships and far more important to know what others need from me if I want to be an effective leader, partner, or communicator.

THE VULNERABLE LEADER

*The difficult thing is that vulnerability is the first thing I
look for in you, and the last thing I am willing to show you.
In you, it's courage and daring. In me, it's weakness.*

—Brené Brown

The origin of the word "personality" is *persona*, a mask. The word
persona literally referred to the distinctive masks that were worn by
actors in the theater of the ancient Greeks. Taking off our carefully
cultivated social masks requires significant vulnerability, so not surprisingly, it takes much courage to do so, especially for leaders.

Along with humility, the courage to be open and the willingness to focus more on the deeper interpersonal needs of those we're
leading lies at the heart of being a "vulnerable leader." This is a
concept, however, that historically, and still for many of us, contra-
dicts the classic image of a strong leader, the more traditional "large
and in charge" leader who often looks and acts more like a stallion
than a mare.

In his newest book on leadership, Tomas Chamorro-Premuzic
delves into the question of whether leaders are born or made. He
cites intelligence as a significant factor along with an abundance of
other factors that include empathy, integrity, and competence. "The
key goal of a leader," he says, "is not to get to the top of a group or an
organization but to help the team outperform its rivals."[2]

Agreed. And one thing we know for sure from our experience
is that *there is no "one size fits all" when it comes to leading.* What we
can say is that the perceptual awareness we glean from an individual's
Birkman helps determine the leader's fit for a specific industry or

2   Tomas Chamorro-Premuzic, *Why Do So Many Incompetent Men Become Leaders? (And
How to Fix It)*. Harvard Business Review Press, 2019.

organizational culture, and while there is no perception or behavior that guarantees leadership success, we can predict *how* that person is most likely to lead and succeed, what they're most likely to emphasize as important, and what kind of overall culture they will be inclined to build. One goal of learning about an individual's perception is to provide clues as to what companies can expect from someone they plan to hire or promote, a factor that becomes especially important when it comes to career pathing or succession planning. As Chamorro-Premuzic writes, "Some characteristics are hard to change. If we want an animal to climb a tree, we are better off finding a squirrel than training a fish."

Through the centuries, as leadership aligned with economic dominance or political power, leaders were equated with military might as they led their troops into battle. They were expected to be brave, assertive, and confident. In my late teen years, feminism and the women's movement was (at least in my perceptions) just beginning to be a hot topic for discussion. Personally, in my early life, I never aspired to lead the Birkman organization. If I thought about it all, I assumed the firm would be run by my dad until a suitable (male) business executive would take over. This was quite okay with me at the time because I was focused on my musical theater interests, my marriage, and raising my family. Life, however, has a way of taking us by surprise and teaching us in unexpected ways.

I am convinced that nothing we learn is ever wasted. What never occurred to me at the time was that directing musical theater projects and leading choirs was teaching me how to better communicate with groups and gain more confidence with teams—showing me how to become more of a "lead mare." As a stage director, I was learning to coach, make production and casting decisions, and referee the interpersonal relationships of the cast. To be sure, more than once, this has proved useful in the corporate world.

Another way I unknowingly prepped for leadership was parenting, probably the most challenging job ever and the "team" you get to manage 'round the clock. It was my responsibility to maintain our household with three offspring while my husband, due to the demands of his job, traveled for weeks, sometimes even months, at a time. Parenting may not typically be regarded as a boot camp for leading a company, but I could argue otherwise. Looking back, I've realized that much of running a business requires similar skills: persistence, patience with people, and common sense as you juggle multiple priorities. While my husband was on the road, it was my job to manage household deadlines (operations), pay taxes and bills (accounting), referee our kids (HR), and work multiple jobs in leading various musical groups.

It was hardly apparent to me at the time, but in the clear lens of life's rearview mirror, those years were teaching me much of what would come in handy for leadership. I suspect this is one reason so many women have found they can successfully transition from managing the family at home to managing their teams at work.

A NEW CHAPTER: MY SECOND CAREER

By 2001, I saw my aging parents struggling with the succession plan for our family business. There had been a revolving door of several presidents who had not proved to be exactly what my founder father was seeking. All in all, it seemed a good time for me to be present on a more regular basis, if only to learn what should come next for the company my parents had spent their lives building.

Without ever discussing it, I think both my father and I just naturally assumed a male businessman would become the next leader. After more than a year of observing, learning by listening, and asking questions, I saw my father continuing to be concerned about who should serve as our next Birkman president. I thought he was about to appoint someone who was a good person but, in my opinion, not our best choice for president. At that point, I brazenly walked in and told him I was ready to shift my energies from music to working full time at Birkman to further his legacy. He looked pleasantly surprised, smiled, and said, *"Really? Are you sure?"*

No, I wasn't all that sure, but society was beginning to be slightly more accepting of women in leadership roles. Since I had grown up with our product and services, and had done as-needed training for the company, I'd been immersed in our subject matter and decided the time was right that I could fully commit myself to learning the "business" side of the business. In April 2002, whether I (or for that matter, our company!) was ready or not, I was given the privilege to begin learning real leadership lessons and knew I'd have to ramp it up to warp speed.

One lesson I've learned is that every company, just like every person, is a dynamic and organic entity. Organizations, regardless of size, change constantly, as they continually contract and expand. As I'd learned in theater, people have their seasons and their roles to play. Employees, design styles, and technologies will come and go, but I believe leadership is, above all, a perpetual balancing act. My job (as lead mare) is to keep us moving to safe and enriching ground and hopefully in a healthy direction. I came late into this second career, and as one who has learned on the job, I consider myself lucky and blessed.

My ambitious self says we could always do much more and far better, but we've stayed successfully afloat through two recessions, and I'm grateful for the opportunity to work with people from all over the world. After nearly two decades of working inside Birkman, I can affirm that each one of my top four Birkman Interests have been applied in one form or another to my job here at the company. I know how fortunate I am to have landed in an encore career that aligns so closely with what I find most exciting and rewarding.

I must admit that there have been many days where I've felt like a misfit, and certainly it was surprising for me to land in a "lead mare" role because I'm in no way what most would regard as a stereotypical leader. It's easy for me to be humble since the only way I *can l*ead is by relying on the strengths of other capable people who do what I cannot do, see things I cannot see, and know things I don't know. I'm convinced successful leaders succeed because they work to identify and surround themselves with the best complementary talent. These are also the leaders who are willing to admit their own vulnerability and "stand on their own inner roots" as they invite others to do the same.

The perceptual awareness we emphasize at Birkman focuses heavily on knowing my own interior roots and what we call the "roots," or motivating Needs, of others. This was the lesson we learned in Arizona when we stopped worrying about ourselves in the arena and focused instead on the needs of the horse. I truly believe most people mean well most of the time in their jobs and relationships, just as I meant well as I tried to lead that horse. The problem was not the horse; it was me. Fretting about how I might fail or being embarrassed about how inept I looked down in that arena may have stressed me out but did nothing to encourage the horse to follow me. The horse was finally able to follow my nonverbal commands once

I *understood the needs of the horse.* Social intelligence attunes us to the needs of others so we can lead them more effectively. As in the natural world, leadership in the business world improves when I'm less concerned about my own ego and image and more concerned about what my team and employees *need from me.*

The deepest principle of human nature is the craving to be appreciated.

—Henry James

Born as social creatures, we are hardwired to instinctively crave the acceptance and approval of our tribes and peers; it's key to our survival. This is one reason we so often hear that many of us struggle with wondering if we're imposters, if we are really "good enough." Indeed, the Birkman itself is built on the concept that most of us are trying our best to "get it right" when it comes to relationships.

Our research is grounded on the tenet that most people will naturally desire to be seen in a positive light, to find acceptance from others, and this is very good for all the industries that make trophies and host award shows. So clearly it's normal for us to fear anything that makes us look too open or too vulnerable. I understand the fear that an assessment like ours, or any assessment, might expose our interpersonal roots in an unfavorable way, especially if I'm in a managerial or leadership position. Be assured, however, the Birkman is an affirming assessment and not an assessment to be feared. If taken sincerely, people need never worry about what it will say since there are widely varying perceptions, but no "wrong" scores.

All experts agree that accurate self-awareness is the first requirement for a good leader, but it is hard for me to turn the perceptual lens on myself. In fact, it's impossible. It is easy to understand why if you think of mirrors. I can see my face in a mirror, but if I want to see what the back of my head looks like, I must turn around and use a second mirror. An assessment like Birkman can serve as that "second mirror" for seeing myself more accurately while also accepting that it's never just about me; it's always about others-awareness and social comprehension as well.

All organizations consist of people who must collaborate in one way or another, so teams (real-time or virtual) remain a primary focus for all businesses, regardless of the industry or the size of the organization. Technology impacts us all at a dizzying pace, but ultimately, it's the people—the interpersonal support and healthy relationships we cultivate that allow us to succeed over time. How often do we still hear this lament: good employees often leave companies, not because they don't like their jobs, but because they don't like their managers.

Just as we learned at the ranch with the horses, I cannot lead or encourage people to perform at their highest levels unless I'm aware of their individual and specific underlying needs, or their motivational "roots." And at the same time, my ability to *sustain* good leadership comes from honoring my own core needs as well. To echo Dr. Brené Brown, true vulnerability is a strength, a strength I'd define as the willingness to be open, to know myself, and to know what I need from others. And remember, these internal, motivating needs can, in fact, be (and will look) very different from one person to the next, from one leader to the next.

What if we all had the courage to "pierce our own shells" and to remove the masks we don't need? What kinds of empathetic leaders of ourselves, our families, and our communities might we become?

TAKEAWAY TIPS

- To effectively lead or communicate, we must know what motivates others and what they are expecting or seeking from us.

- We can build stronger bridges for connection when we share our hidden but powerful interior Needs (our root systems).

- Becoming vulnerable, or "piercing the shell," enables us to empower other people by modeling the way. When we stand on and share our own motivating "roots," others know it's safe to share their interpersonal Needs as well.

CHAPTER 3

THE SCIENCE OF SOCIAL COMPREHENSION

Why Perceptions Dominate

Could a greater miracle take place than for us to
look through each other's eyes for an instant?
—Henry David Thoreau, *Walden*

n 2014, as several members of the Birkman team and I prepped for
our first trip to the Middle East, we were told we'd need a screen in
the center of the room to separate the women from the men. This was
a state-mandated requirement, and though unusual for us, it was at
that time a cultural expectation. My Houston team was already a little
nervous about training in a place so distant and unfamiliar. Our local
representative, however, was quick to assure us all would be well. I tried
to calm my own concerns, but we spoke no Arabic, and frankly, while
it was exciting to enter a new market, I had some anxiety about training
in a culture where the gender roles were so different from our own.

A brief, touristy stopover in Dubai helped us recover from the long flight. We shopped there at the gargantuan Mall of the Emirates for suitable abayas (robes) and lovely head scarves before flying on to Saudi Arabia to train thirty new Arabic-speaking consultants in the Birkman Method. On the first day of the four-day training, the hotel provided four portable screens to divide the room into the female side and the male side. As facilitators, we stood at the front where it was easy to us to see both sides, and in short order, we got used to the screens. The pace had to be slowed to allow time for translating, but we soon forgot our initial concerns as we related to the people in the room. Soon there was connection, and the fifteen men and fifteen women in the room were being perceived by us as approachable human beings who had their own personal realities and interesting stories.

We continued to bond as the week progressed, each day growing more comfortable with one another. We realized that our trainees, in a surprising symbol of trust and confidence, had begun to remove one screen per day, and by the final day, only one "required" screen remained.

Prior to our arrival, each participant had completed our online assessment, which interprets complex perceptions and personality traits through words and a simple, visual format. Nine interpersonal energies or, as we call them, motivational Components, address behaviors on multiple levels, and our job was to show these coaches and organizational experts how to use and interpret them. By the third day, as we addressed their socialized behaviors one by one, it was not difficult to see how men compared to women in this group—after all, the room itself was divided. That afternoon we came to the Birkman Component we call Assertiveness, which measures verbal dominance or giving and receiving communication in a direct and verbally dominant way. When this Component is high, the person is comfortable with speaking up readily, even forcefully, in social situations.

As we discussed the relative scores and percentages for the participants in the room, there was a startling discovery. If you'd asked me before we arrived in Saudi to predict, I'd have guessed the men would show up as being more assertive. Metrics for this group, however, showed that the *women in* the room averaged as *more verbally assertive.* These ladies were reporting that they were more comfortable in speaking up and speaking out than the men in the room. Despite the media stereotype I'd held of Middle Eastern women, so modestly draped in their dark robes and hijabs, this group of ladies showed up as more willing to be assertive and *verbally dominant* than the men in our room. So much for assumptions, stereotypes, and biases!

Next, we discussed the behavioral trait we call Emotional Energy. This Birkman Component measures how *emotionally expressive* we tend to be and addresses our comfort levels with outward displays of emotion.

Here, I must admit, we had another surprise. This time, the *men in the group* averaged *higher than the women* in their responses. At least for this group, the men were refuting the common assumption that women are always more emotional than men. When we shared this insight with our trainees, one of the men cheerfully piped over the screen, "See, ladies, we do have feelings!" The entire room erupted in laughter, and in that moment, we could have been

WE'D BEEN UNITED OVER THOSE DAYS IN A PROFOUNDLY HUMAN WAY, A WAY THAT OVERCAME ANY SCREENS OR STEREOTYPES DESIGNED TO SEPARATE.

in any city, in any country. Connected even more tightly by what we'd just learned, we'd begun to see each other in whole new ways. We'd been united over those days in a profoundly human way, a way that overcame any screens or stereotypes designed to separate.

This was my first visit to the Middle East, but it was not my last. In my most recent visit in late 2017, we heard about the ways the new crown prince was planning significant changes with his Saudi Vision 2030 initiative. He'd already removed the mandate for gender-separating screens and would soon allow women to drive. Despite the changes now taking place in Saudi Arabia, I'm grateful for the lessons I learned from that opportunity to visit before they were changed.

IMPLICIT BIAS?

For me, that first visit to the Middle East was a revelation. From years of only viewing the Middle East from my Western perspective, I assumed that requiring women to cover made them feel dominated or suppressed. This might be true at times and for some women, but speaking directly with these ladies and seeing their psychological data had framed the ancient covering tradition in a very different light for me, a light that exposed my own misperceptions. The ladies told us that the practice of covering when in public often made them feel safer, was frequently done out of respect for their husbands, and frankly, from a practical standpoint, helped protect their skin from the relentless desert sun. In fact, the abayas these ladies wore in our classes were graceful, elegant robes with a wide variety of styling details and design. As a Westerner, I must confess that wearing an abaya for our training was also supercomfortable and convenient!

By the time we returned in late 2017, some significant changes had already occurred. This time, I was in Riyadh to speak at a Birkman Conference. There were no screens down the middle of the large meeting space, as it was no longer a state requirement to separate men and women. What was interesting was to see that, even without screens, the men and women still *chose* to sit mostly segregated. However, this time it was a voluntary decision, and whether based on cultural habit or long-standing tradition, it was good to be reminded of what I should have guessed: these women were not what I'd perceived them to be from afar, and the men, of course, "did have feelings." Certainly not all the Saudi men were more assertive than the women. It can be all too tempting in an unfamiliar situation to fall back on unconscious biases and stereotypes. What I learned again that day was that my perceptions had in fact been *misperceptions*, and these biases can all too easily become barriers to true human connection.

We'll talk more about interpersonal cultural differences in later chapters, but this travel story taught me an important lesson. Our research continues to affirm that we cannot assume one generation, gender, or culture has "more of or less than" when it comes to feelings or sensitivity. We've been monitoring this for years, but the gender differences we're seeing throughout our database are minimal. Men may have been *taught to appear* outwardly objective, but their internal feelings *can and do* run deep. Conversely, women often say they can be made to feel "too bossy" if they appear more verbally dominant or assertive than we expect they should be. It's my conviction that these common assumptions are based primarily on our culturally defined roles, and mostly, they are *learned* behaviors. As cultures evolve, these aspects of our behaviors can shift and can be seen differently.

In Riyadh, the Saudi group saw how the ways they'd learned to show up in their day-to-day relationships combined seamlessly with the ways they were hardwired from birth to behave. In other words, as with any group of people anywhere in the world, they were able to understand how their external "learned and adaptable" social styles worked in sync with the internal motivations they'd had from birth. These traits and perceptions are not culture or gender specific; they are human.

And here's the very good news: there is no one "better than" or "more normal" set of scores when it comes to the way we measure interpersonal Components. We all have perceptions and traits that are as unique as our own DNA. However, what *is* dangerous for us is to judge others by our own expectations and assumptions. It is dangerous to hold others to our own perceptions of how they *should* feel or what they *should* need.

I'm grateful for the opportunities I've had to travel and to witness such a variety of people through our Birkman lens. When you visit a new place or live for a while in a new culture, it's fascinating to see how varied we really are and how different we often appear. These variations make travel fun to experience, but the majority of these (apparent) differences are not the distinctions we were born with; they're ways we adapt to our own "tribes" and how our social system teaches us to behave if we want to fit in. Most traditions and cultural distinctions therefore are *learned behaviors*. These learned behaviors are influenced by many factors, passed from generation to generation, and they matter. However, when you adjust to outward differences in language, customs, and dress, when you drill down to the fundamental core of being human, we humans appear to be remarkably similar in our perceptions, motivations, and emotions.

Each of us is clearly a one-of-a-kind individual. The tricky part about getting along with others is that, despite all our contrasting perceptions and differing styles, we absolutely must figure out how to transcend our differences, and as David Rakoff writes, "still we must come together." Our planet, our individual and communal survival, depends on it. Over the centuries, when we weren't finding new and clever ways to destroy our neighbors, we occasionally sought better ways to understand them. While we've found it *necessary* to coexist, we've never found it *easy*. In the next chapters, we'll consider some social science factors that make communicating such an ongoing challenge. We'll also explore one of the reasons getting along with others, difficult though it may be, is vital for us in every walk of life.

MORE DIVERSITY WITHIN THAN BETWEEN

In 2002, as I was starting my tenure, the Birkman questionnaire was available in only a handful of languages. Since then, we've translated the Birkman questionnaire into twenty-five languages, and I'm eager to add more. What I see as reassuring

THERE IS MORE DIVERSITY WITHIN A CULTURE THAN THERE IS BETWEEN CULTURES.

and exciting is the way Birkman tracks across global cultures. Over decades of collecting empirical data at Birkman, we've seen how our personalities and cultures differ and the ways they're the same. And over the years, what our research continues to say is that there is more diversity *within* a culture than there is *between* cultures, adding even more weight to poet Maya Angelou's statement: "We are more alike, my friends, than we are unalike."[3] This makes sense to me because I believe that the diversity within each culture is vitally important. Our individual diversity of interests and personality is there for a reason. It's there because it's necessary. We *need others* who possess talents and interests that contrast with our own and whose talents and interests round out the needs of the community, the office, or

---

3   Maya Angelou, "Human Family" from *I Shall Not Be Moved*. New York: Bantam, 1990.

the team. When scientists dissected the human genome, they discovered that our genetic DNA is 99.9 percent the same for all Homo sapiens.[4] When I heard this years ago, it proved for me that all of us (no matter the race or gender) have even more in common than we thought. The genome discovery also proved that the tiny sliver of diversity we *do* possess is significant and becomes incredibly important. This natural diversity in each of us and throughout our cultures is the very thing that enables our shared survival.

I believe it's our natural, hardwired perceptions combined with our learned, adaptive insights that influence how we see others and how we learn to differentiate ourselves. From what we're learning, it seems obvious that a certain amount of what we term "personality," along with what we enjoy and find interesting to do, are innate parts of how we arrived in the world. If you're not too sure about this, ask anyone who's been a parent. From their first cry, babies seem to arrive preloaded with certain interests and traits that came with their own unique DNA. It makes perfect sense. Natural diversity has served and saved our tribes over the centuries, and in these times, it serves and saves our teams and organizations.

It doesn't take much imagination to consider what a disaster it would be if we all had identical interests and the same career aspirations. Our inborn differences bring the essential diversity we need to survive and thrive, something we'll examine more closely in chapter 8. Whether it's the office team, the city council, or the school board, we're clearly interdependent. This is the nonnegotiable reason we must collaborate and get along. We do this a lot better when we understand how we're *usefully* different!

---

4   National Human Genome Research Institute, "Genetics vs. Genomics Fact Sheet," accessed October 14, 2019, https://www.genome.gov/about-genomics/fact-sheets/ Genetics-vs-Genomics.

The fact is, we all have at least this one thing in common: we each see the world through our own personal lens and filters. At Birkman, we report the perceptions people have of themselves and the way they expect others in the world to be. Through our multidimensional approach, behavioral traits and career strengths are seen together in a nuanced and complex portrait. Since

THROUGH OUR MULTIDIMENSIONAL APPROACH, BEHAVIORAL TRAITS AND CAREER STRENGTHS ARE SEEN TOGETHER IN A NUANCED AND COMPLEX PORTRAIT.

many aspects of personality cannot be seen from outward behaviors, these unseen traits can be blind spots for us and a source of confusion and frustration for others. As we'll examine in later chapters, uncovering these "hidden" aspects of our own personalities and the "unexpected" perceptions of others is a powerful tool for personal development and building healthier relationships.

* * *

Do people change? And if so, how much and in what ways?

If we accept that a certain amount of what's referred to as "personality" is definitely born into us, what about the many ways we *can and do change* or adapt? What about our freedom to learn, mature, and make choices for personal development?

Well … yes! Happily, while we're born with certain interests and traits, we humans also have free will. This enables us to learn, evolve, and continually make better choices, so there are many parts of our nature we *can* change. This is the reason self-help books will continue to be written and coaching is here to stay. We are in business because we know for sure that people *can* and do evolve to become better versions of themselves. There's no question we can choose to improve over time and that we share a remarkable ability to adapt to others in our social environment. Carl Jung, who famously brought many of the concepts of today's social psychology into more modern thinking, theorized that personality arises "for reasons of adaptation or personal convenience."[5] We agree, and this is supported by our current social science data. While it's easy to see the superficial differences among us—age, race, gender, socioeconomics—it's important to know that every field of research and social science affirms the common threads we share in our variegated human tapestry. In all our astonishing variety, we are in fact, one.

Tempting though it is to buy into the myth of separateness, the science continues to show we're far more alike than we realize—not only in our genetics and basic personality types, but also in our core humanness. Once more, *why* we need to connect is obvious: we *need* each other. Period, full stop.

Then the next question has to be "How?" How do we connect? How do we find ways to do a better job of noticing, appreciating, and being there for one another? How do we address the ongoing challenges of understanding personality differences and do a better job of getting along? This book will highlight some of the ways social psychology can enable us to forgive more and wound less as we move in closer to understand our fellow *creatures of contact*. When we succeed in doing this, our days really can be brighter, our relationships healthier.

---

5   Carl Jung, *Collected Works of C. G. Jung, Volume 6: Psychological Types*. Edited by R. F. C. Hull. Translated by Gerhard Adler. Princeton, NJ: Princeton University Press, 2014.

Birkman training in Riyadh, Saudi Arabia, 2014

TAKEAWAY TIPS

- We see others through our own perceptual filters and these perceptions create our own individual and subjective reality.

- Perceptions of self and others work in tandem to inform what others would term our "personality."

- Social perceptions are varied, complex, and multidimensional, but the better we understand these perceptions the easier it becomes to build trust and heal divisions.

CHAPTER 4

CAPTURING THE POWER OF PERCEPTIONS

The reality of life is that your perceptions—right or wrong—influence everything else you do. When you get a proper perspective of your perceptions, you may be surprised how many other things fall into place.

—Roger W. Birkman

I f you ask me to describe our assessment, I would say Birkman is first and foremost a *perceptual* analysis. Throughout our long history, we've seen that how we view ourselves, along with how we perceive others, takes center stage in determining who we are and how we behave. The power of social perceptions came into sharp focus for my father when he flew bombing missions during the Second World War.

In the cold, dark predawn hours of May 27, 1944, pilot Roger Birkman suited up with his crew of nine to fly a B-17 bomber on their nineteenth mission. This time would be different. As they returned to the base in England, the German Luftwaffe managed to set the plane on fire over Belgium. As the pilot, Lt. Birkman was required to jump last. He'd later recall that there had been no time for paratrooper training, but his rigger had packed the parachute well, and a burning plane is good inspiration to jump. He plunged into a barley field with only a badly sprained ankle, and, as the occupying Nazi soldiers poked through the fields searching for the downed crew, the American pilot held his breath … and prayed.

He hid for a while in a haystack under a small shed that belonged to a farmer's family until the Belgian Resistance could hatch a plan to rescue him. They brought him some peasant farmer clothes, hid his bomber jacket and uniform, and ferreted him to safety on a bicycle built for two. A member of the Belgian Resistance pedaled him to the townhome of a wealthy factory owner in the tiny village of Sint Niklaas (Saint Nicholas) where George and Marie Smet lived. A childless couple in their fifties, the Smets were willing to brave the terrible dangers of hiding my father and welcomed him like a son until he could be rescued with the Allied liberation of Europe. Fortunately, his entire crew survived what had become their final mission of the war. This experience put into motion Roger Birkman's unrelenting curiosity for how perceptions play out when it comes to understanding people.

At the end of every bombing mission, the crew was required to participate in the compulsory debrief that followed each military operation. Roger Birkman, always a good listener and keen observer of people, noticed something important: each crew member's retelling of the mission was uniquely his own. Because he knew each man so well, he saw how their individual backgrounds, priorities, values, and fears impacted their perceptions of reality. They'd all experienced the same event, yet each recounted it somewhat differently. How interesting that each man told the story in a way

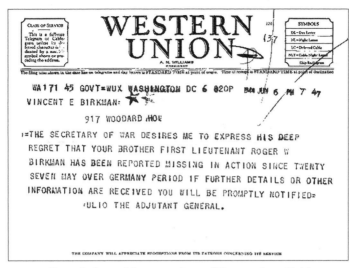

Roger Birkman Missing in Action Telegram, June 1944

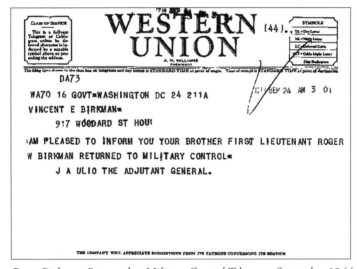

Roger Birkman Returned to Military Control Telegram, September 1944

that was technically correct, yet each crew member's perceptions of the bombing mission, and of one another, were different. Each man described the mission through the filters of his own personal and subjective reality. These wartime observations on the power of perception became a catalyst for Roger Birkman's early research and the discoveries that were to come.

Roger Birkman (kneeling, second from left) and his crew preparing for flight, 1944

Ever curious about people, Birkman wondered: *Why do their perceptions vary and contrast to such a degree? And if they do vary, why is this significant? Is this showing us something profound about our own diverse personalities and behaviors?*

Each member of his crew had recounted his individual reality, which my father understood was their own personal truth. He continued to ponder these questions, and when the war was over, the returning pilot faced a difficult decision. Should he accept his pastor father's assumption that he'd study theology like the six generations of Lutheran pastors before him? Or, thanks to the GI Bill, pursue the emerging field of social psychology that had begun to beckon so brightly? At a deep personal level, Roger Birkman now saw social psychology as his spiritual calling. Rather than studying to become a pastor, he channeled his faith into a desire to help people in this new and exciting way. His wartime memories of perception stimulated his thinking about how to truly and better understand other people— the beginning of his lifelong pursuit of what he would term "social comprehension."

For his initial research, he interviewed people by asking them questions about their jobs, their experiences, and their worldview. He questioned anyone who was willing to be interviewed: managers, teachers, salespeople, engineers, accountants. Again he was impressed by the lack of alignment in how people perceived the same things. With an empirical approach, his theories on perception began to take shape. He realized the significant and often detrimental impact our deep-seated social perceptions have on all our relationships and made it his mission to help people understand how their perceptions inform their own realities, just as he'd seen with the men in his crew.

To this day, Birkman's approach is distinguished by the fact that it taps into understanding the value and importance of perceptions: what a person expects and how they experience the world around them in combination with how they perceive themselves. Once we can clearly see how our own perceptions contrast or align with others, it's easier to minimize defensiveness and easier to empathize.

DO YOU SEE WHAT I SEE?

Throughout my father's ninety-five years, *perception* more so than "personality" remained a favorite word of his. He realized that it's our contrasting, sometimes clashing, perceptions that often make communication difficult. Throughout his life, my father was convinced that heightened social comprehension was key to unlocking our ability to communicate more effectively. If we could understand more about how our perceptions influence all our relationships, we could do a better job of getting along with others. The ability to see (perceive) self and others more clearly often determines success or failure in all our relationships, and this is the reason he focused so intently on their power. The way we see ourselves and how we expect the world to be influences how we behave and interact in every relationship we value—whether at work or at home.

When we can more accurately perceive the world through the eyes of the other person, even for a moment, we're empowered to relate to them in better ways. To be precise, we can communicate and work with others according to what aligns with *their* perceptual needs, rather than relying solely on our own. As demonstrated by what we learned at the ranch in Arizona, we did a much better job of getting the horses to follow us as soon as we were told what the horse needed and expected from us.

When my dad did his initial research, the concept of focusing on the needs of the "other" as well as the needs of the self sounded simple enough, but in the emerging field of social psychology it was a startling new concept. His method emphasizes the constant interplay of relational dynamics between individuals. What we as humans all share is a fundamental desire to be seen, to be noticed, and ideally, to be sympathetically understood by others. Gaining a clear awareness of my own style is often helpful but is seldom a surprise. However, when I combine self-awareness with how I view others and expect others to be, it brings powerful insights that, when applied, can enhance social/emotional intelligence.

These objective insights are designed to diminish the judgment factor because there are no better or worse perceptions, just different and contrasting ones. Once you tap into the complexity of relational and motivational perceptions, you begin to understand people in a multidimensional way, as if seeing through both eyes. By wearing Birkman glasses, we can work together according to what best motivates the other person. This is how Birkman insights shine brighter lights on the normal complexity of our visible and invisible perceptions. Birkman has stayed the course over the decades because this kind of self-understanding and people knowledge paves the way to greater emotional intelligence, enhanced job performance, and heightened leadership acumen.

Late in his life, when my father was still working in the office with us, I was impressed by the story of a woman who'd been born cross-eyed, but after therapeutic treatment, was able to gain stereopsis, or depth perception. Suddenly, with this added dimension to her vision, the way she saw everything was totally transformed. "I was startled by my view of falling snow," she recalled. "The large wet flakes were floating about me in a graceful, three-dimensional dance ... "[6] This was because, at long last, she saw that snowflakes had depth and dimension, that they were not flat objects. For the first time in her life, both of her eyes—one for distance, one for close-up—were finally working in sync. This duality of seeing through both eyes gave her 3-D depth perception for the very first time in her life, radically changing her perception of the world.

When I heard her story, I raced into his office to tell my dad this was analogous to what he'd been doing over the decades with social comprehension. Looking at behaviors through the Birkman lenses, we gain depth perception on people. We don't focus only on the view of self, but factor together our career interests, along with our social perceptions and expectations of self and others. This allows us to see ourselves *and others* in 3-D, more clearly and more appreciatively.

* * *

---

6   Susan Barry, *Fixing My Gaze: A Scientist's Journey into Seeing in Three Dimensions.* New York: Basic Books, 2009.

In choosing social psychology, Roger Birkman's deepest desire was to help people appreciate how their personal hardwired DNA—their motivating perceptions—determined their uniqueness and shaped their comprehension of the world. He was convinced that when you get a better handle on how these perceptions play out, you can be more content, more engaged, and more productive in all aspects of your life.

> **IT IS NOT LIKELY THAT OUR EXPERIENCES SHAPE OUR PERCEPTION, RATHER THAT IT IS MORE OFTEN OUR PERCEPTIONS THAT CREATE OUR EXPERIENCES.**

He generally preferred to downplay the word *personality* in favor of *perceptions*—the perceptions that open the eyes of awareness to how our overall interpersonal perceptions impact all our relationships, everything we say and do.

Based on his WWII experiences, Roger Birkman had witnessed firsthand the powerful way individual perceptions impact our realities. In his doctoral dissertation, when he documented the differing perceptions of his crew members, he mentioned that sometimes a mountain and a cloud bank were indistinguishable when flying, describing them as sometimes appearing "illusory, irrational, and unreal, and yet they were real to the person, and as such, influenced their behaviors."[7] Building on this discovery, he unlocked new insights into human personality and social science with research that concluded, paradoxically, that it is not likely that our *experiences shape our perception,* rather that it is more often our *perceptions that create our experiences.*

What I am still hearing from many organizational experts today is the notion that we can place ourselves in one of three distinct categories

---

7   Roger Birkman, "Test of Social Comprehension," (PhD diss., University of Texas, 1961).

and classify ourselves as an introvert, an extrovert, or a combination of the two: an ambivert.

While it's true that most of us lean strongly in the direction of being either *more introverted* or *more extroverted*, I believe that the majority of us are more accurately described as ambiverts. The father of modern psychology, Carl Jung, declared there is no such thing as a person who is 100 percent introvert or 100 percent extrovert. Factoring in the reality that Birkman was originally designed for people in the workplace, this certainly appears to be true.

While we may lean predominantly in one direction or the other, no functioning person, if you look carefully through our Birkman lens, is entirely one or entirely the other. What we can see clearly on a Birkman report is the subtle and nuanced ways most of us are widely varying blends of ambiversion. In some areas of our behaviors, we may show up as more typically extroverted, and in other areas of our Birkman, we can possess attributes of our more introverted talents— and all this quite naturally displayed within the same individual. Even with a specific Birkman Component, we can and frequently do register on the Birkman as a blend or combination of the two. While many of us, if asked, may find ourselves identifying more easily with the introversion or extroversion qualities in ourselves, our years of data show that we humans are quite literally all over the map in our ambiversion variety!

Here's one example of an executive with an "unexpected" trait that I recently encountered while facilitating a workshop for women leaders who all owned and ran companies well in excess of $50 million. Of the group of eighteen, if you observed our day-long session, you'd say most of them appeared to be gregarious and confident extroverts. The youngest executive that day was a third-generation leader who had been quiet and reserved throughout the morning session. She was obviously an introvert, and we were all aware of this. In fact, we could easily see this reflected in the Birkman reporting she shared with the group. She ranked high on most of our introversion scales, and her quiet, restrained demeanor certainly backed that up.

At the lunch break, when the others had left the room, she walked over to me and confided: "I have an issue." It's significant to note she did not bring this up in front of the entire group but waited to speak with me one to one, the way most introverts prefer to relate. She said, "I need to ask you about something. I find that too many times when I'm meeting with one or more of my team, I can too quickly start to dominate or 'bulldoze' the conversation."

I glanced at her Assertiveness numbers and saw they were, in fact, much higher than one might expect, especially given the fact that overall she was such an intensely introverted leader. Assertiveness on the Birkman is just what it sounds like: rarely an introversion trait but a characteristic associated more often with extroversion. Seeing on paper that she had this unexpected trait (one that she could certainly use to her advantage if she managed it well!) was an important eye-opener for this young CEO. One of the more fascinating discoveries we regularly witness with people are the subtle and unexpected aspects of their perceptions—and these unexpected combinations are exactly what makes them uniquely who they are.

Similar stories, in different ways, applied to each of the successful leaders that day. We could walk them through all their scores, and for each of the Birkman Components, we could say, "Here, you show up in a more introverted way, and in this other way, your team will see you as more of an extrovert." Or, as often occurs, we could tell them, "Here, you show up as highly extroverted in your leadership style; however, people may often misperceive you. There's a very good possibility your team is unaware of the areas where your expectations and interior needs are deeply introverted."

Unquestionably, each woman leader in that session had been highly successful in her own way. Like most of us, they were all ambiverts in their own diverse ways. Whether we lean harder toward the introversion side or the extroversion side of the equation, with Birkman we see how certain aspects of our personality cross back and forth across the introvert/extrovert lines to make the majority of us interesting "ambiverts"—each of us in our own individual way.

Of course, it's our outward (what we call "Usual") behaviors that people see from us most of the time. All Usual behaviors are described in positive and socially desirable terms. And they *usually* are positive, except when they are overused or misdirected, or when we encounter periods of prolonged stress and our core Needs go unmet. As we'll discuss later, if we fall into our *distress* default mode, it is unfortunately our friends, family, and coworkers who are subjected to it. Unlike the way we affirmatively describe the "Usual" visible behavior, these frustrated stress behaviors are counterproductive. Sadly, these conditional *distress* behaviors are easy for others to see and are uncomfortable for us. Our Birkman "Stress" behaviors are never fun and never pretty.

If we recognize our Stress behaviors kicking in, the goal is to deploy self-awareness to minimize the damage from our blind spots and do some preventive self-management. Life will always have a way of taking its toll on us, but sharper awareness certainly helps with self-management. Human interaction is challenging precisely because it's perfectly normal for people to be far more complex than their socialized outward behavior indicates. In this way, we can all benefit from "social awareness" glasses to help us better manage ourselves and view one another with greater clarity and compassion.

I once heard an estimate that, in English alone, over two hundred thousand books have been written on leadership. New ones arrive daily, and whatever the total, there is one thing all books on leadership have in common. In one way or another, they all agree that the first requirement for good leadership is becoming self-aware. This is true, of course, but awareness cannot stop with me. Our overarching goal with Birkman data is to shine a brighter light on the need for *others-awareness, in addition to self-awareness.* Self-management is the first step for leaders, but to become a higher-level leader, we must elevate self-awareness to include social savvy and empathetic relational skills.

You and I are a fascinating blend of how we show up day to day to get things done, and these innate traits and behaviors work in tandem with the deeper essence of who we are inside. You are not, and have never been, one-dimensional. How you see yourself, what you most enjoy doing, and how you perceive others is what makes you complex and, without a doubt, unrepeatable.

In a blog by Karen Ehman[8] titled "The three most common reasons for conflict in marriage—they aren't what you think!" she puts forward a compelling case that it's not what most of us would guess. Money? Sex? In-laws? Parenting? Competing with technology for attention? Instead Ehman suggests that the top trio for conflict is emotional baggage, *unmet expectations, and untrue perceptions …* these are the three "that cause communication to derail and send any hopes of harmony packing." She concludes her article by suggesting, "Grant grace and don't give it an expiration date."

---

8   Karen Ehman, "The three most common reasons for conflict in marriage—they aren't what you think!" Fox News, February 24, 2019, https://www.foxnews.com/opinion/the-three-most-common-reasons-for-conflict-in-marriage-they-arent-what-you-think.

FLYING BLIND

At this point in time, I cannot write a book about perceptions and personal truths without also addressing the news and social media's role in our current contentious realities. Understanding the difference between objective reality and subjective reality is a vital distinction to make in our culture. Watch one cable news network for a while, and you're told one thing is "true"; however, if you watch a different network, you're given an entirely different version of the "truth." Ostensibly, both networks are weighing in on the same facts, but with entirely different perceptions of the same "facts." As truth seekers in an age of opinions and misinformation, we have a responsibility to understand that we will all perceive information through our own filters and in our own ways. That uniqueness—the lens we're seeing through—informs our reality. Now more than ever, as opinions frequently overtake and often replace ethical journalism, it helps to keep this in mind. Those who hold opposite political views can argue all day long using the same facts, but their perceptual realities are totally different, and you can't change someone else's personal reality—possibly something to consider if this happens to impact your friends or threatens the peace at a family event.

Rather than believing it's merely a crisis of ideology, I see it as a crisis of perception. If I expect people to share my views, which I perceive as correct and quite obviously true, it surprises me when they disagree. But if I can move in close enough to see from their vantage point, maybe their ideas won't seem so outrageous after all. Even those whose statements make me cringe deserve an effort to pay attention to what might be driving their perceptions. I confess to be preaching to myself as well, but I believe we desperately need resources and the will to rise above the current discord. Our strength as a nation resides in our Founding Fathers' belief in "e pluribus unum" (out of many, one), and we must work harder to live up to the "United" in our name and strive to better connect, even when we don't agree.

Pay attention to paying attention.
The social brain is wired to connect.

—Daniel Goleman,
psychologist and author of *Emotional Intelligence*

On a recent trip to a conference in Virginia, a driver picked me up at the Norfolk airport for a late afternoon commute into Williamsburg. As we drove, I stayed quiet because he'd begun to speak heatedly of his political views, views he and I did not share. For quite a while, I sat tight-lipped in the back seat thinking: *How long is this drive anyway? How long do I have to endure this man's rant?*

Then, remembering I was halfway through writing a book about compassion and connection, I resolved to try a little harder to remind myself that even though I perceived this man as annoying, I should make an effort to honor his "unrepeatable humanity." Taking a deep breath, I began to ask him some questions about himself. When he explained how he'd been a military submarine helmsman, I suddenly became less annoyed and a lot more interested. At that point, it was easy to sincerely thank him for his service to our country. In the next few moments, his rhetoric softened as he talked proudly about having his chauffeuring business, his family, and his hopes for their futures.

Whether I agreed or not, in this man's perceptions at least, his political leanings aligned with his dedication to his family—and this was something we genuinely shared. I still didn't agree with his politics but could begin to see him as a fellow human—a citizen, a veteran, a husband struggling with his family's economic needs—and he was sharing his dreams and fears. As for me, I know I'm still a work in progress, but I'm trying to do a better job of learning patience and honoring someone else's perceptions—even when they clash with my own.

Those years ago, when I first heard Rakoff read his poem, a line that especially stood out for me was *"I think what it means is that central to living a life that is good is a life that's forgiving."* The rancorous political divide we're suffering gives the poet's message even greater resonance for me these days. The more divided we become, the more we can make use of some positive social psychology to remind us of our need for connection. Meanwhile, I'll keep working to become a better listener and hopefully try harder to move in closer to see the world from the vantage point of the other.

In the final decade of his life, we took my dad to fly once again in a restored B-17 bomber like the one he piloted in WWII. As one who'd only flown in commercial airplanes, when we climbed inside the hull of the aircraft, I found it to be shockingly austere: no upholstery or padding, only some plain wooden benches and a large machine gun with a long string of bullets, certainly no amenities. This bomber was built strictly for function. Climbing awkwardly through the cabin and into the cockpit, I saw there was no radar or modern instrumentation panel. Dad told me that when the bombers left their base in England, if one of the planes was shot down, their orders were to fill in quickly for the missing plane and keep flying in formation. "How did you stay in formation," I asked, "with no radar to assist you?"

"With our eyes," he replied matter-of-factly. "We just used our eyes and looked out the windows. And since our eyesight was all we had, the most dangerous time for us to fly was at dusk. When it was getting dark, it was very hard to determine whether it was a cloud bank we were approaching or the side of a mountain. You couldn't always trust what you were seeing." Clearly, perceptions matter.

My dad was a pilot who had to make life-or-death decisions based on fleeting perceptions, but when it comes to perceiving others, each of us is flying blind. What you see as a cloud might look like a mountain to me. In misreading the reality, in getting caught up in our own subjective perceptions, it's easy to get ourselves in trouble. To avoid this danger, we need ways to see others more accurately. This is possible when we link our own perceptions to the ways others who matter to us see their worlds. In this way we do better self-care and achieve healthier contact and connection with others. When we do it well, there can be a shared reverence for the other and deeper appreciation for our own "unrepeatable humanness."

Roger Birkman, 1944

B-17 bombers, as flown by Roger Birkman

TAKEAWAY TIPS

- Needs are the internal expectations and motivators that allow us to feel secure and fulfilled. They are our internal "comfort zones."

- For most people, their internal Needs will be different from their outward behaviors, and Needs are not easily seen.

- Interpersonal Needs play out in the relationships we have with other people. It requires work on our part to ensure these Needs are met and that we understand the innermost Needs of those who matter to us.

CHAPTER 5

NO TREE STANDS ALONE

Maybe you are searching among the branches,
for what only appears in the roots.

—**Rumi**

As a confessed tree hugger, I've always loved trees. Perhaps because I have always lived in such a hot climate, I value their shade and diverse beauty. An early childhood memory was to climb the gnarly old Chinese tallow trees in our apartment complex. It made me feel on top of the world! Now, as a grandmother, I aim to plant as many trees as I can for the next generations to climb.

Toward this goal, my husband and I have planted many young oaks in our yard, adding to the ancient live oaks that have survived Gulf storms and hurricanes for over a century. Last summer, in advance of the hurricane season, we hired an arborist to check the health of our massive old oaks. After inspecting the trees, he reassured us we needn't worry about one of these behemoths crashing onto our roof. "Their roots are so deeply intertwined and interconnected that their root system anchors them all," he said. "Even if one of these trees were to fall in a storm, the other oaks would support it, they'd be able to hold it up." Teamwork in nature.

One of the best ways for me to describe our interpersonal Needs has always been the metaphor of trees. When I explain that the "Usual" observable parts of our temperament are like the part of the tree from the ground up with its hidden roots functioning like our inner Needs, not easily seen but very important, it's easy for most people to understand how Birkman's Usual and Needs work in sync.

Trees are interconnected organisms that provide the oxygen we need and recently, biological scientists learned they can go a step further. Trees can collaborate. It seems they share with us an ability to communicate with and support the needs of other trees. Canadian arborist and ecologist Suzanne Simard's recent research in the Pacific Northwest proves that trees are able to communicate with one another. Her research revealed that birches communicate through their complex root system, and when needed, they can even share carbon dioxide among themselves.

HER CONCLUSION IS THIS: EVERYTHING THAT LIVES, CONNECTS. EVERYTHING.

Simard explains in her documentary *Do Trees Communicate?* that rather than competing for survival, trees will share carbon dioxide as needed by the other trees. They use underground fungi networks to share resources with one another, and these below ground systems can support each single tree and the entire forest. Her conclusion is this: *everything that lives, connects.*

Everything.

Like humans, trees can also adapt. Plants and trees, with their contrasting needs, are equipped to survive all kinds of climates and environments: cacti thrive in hot arid soil and evergreens in cool, moist climates. With plants or trees and their differing needs, we know there's no better or worse—just different. No judgment. We don't criticize an orchid for needing scant water or denounce the hibiscus for wanting a lot of water. They simply differ in their biological needs, and if we want them to flourish, we must recognize what they need.

This gets harder to do when it comes to people since our human interpersonal Needs are invisible and our "roots" are mostly hidden. It's very easy to misperceive when the other person's Needs are opposite from our own. Conveniently, trees and plants often come with care instructions. People rarely do (unless of course, you have access to their Birkman Report!).

Our interpersonal Needs can be hard to discern unless you know someone well and over time. Even then, we've seen some "aha" moments between couples who've been together for years or between colleagues who've worked together for a long time. When they see their Needs spelled out on a Birkman, they tell us they've learned something they hadn't known or understood before about their longstanding relationship.

Our interpersonal Needs or individual "Care Instructions" range a wide spectrum. They are as different for people as the watering needs are for plants. What makes one plant thrive can wither another, and what recharges one person can exhaust the other.

This is a common and very likely scenario: because I don't know what your Needs are, based on my own perceptions, I am going to naturally assume that your Needs are the same as mine. After all, why *wouldn't* you want what I want? Why wouldn't you see things as I see them? It's the golden rule after all—to be kind, I should treat you as I want to be treated, right?

The golden rule works beautifully in most situations, but not consistently when it comes to social interaction. In fact, our statistics say if I treat you as I want to be treated, I'd be wrong much of the time. What our database affirms is that the overwhelming majority of the time, a person's internal Needs will differ, to a greater or lesser degree, from their outward behaviors and demeanor. Based on our own data science, this will occur between 70 and 99 percent of the time. We therefore suggest a platinum rule: aim to go beyond your own Needs. Recognize *their* Needs.

Heidi Grant makes an excellent point in her TED talk about a concept she calls "the illusion of transparency." She explains that we tend to believe other people *should be able to see or interpret our Needs and feelings*, that the way we perceive things should be clear to them. After all, if we can feel it, and we can see it, why don't they? The ever-confounding reality is this—they do not and they cannot. Much as we'd like to be able to, we cannot "read people's minds" or accurately intuit their perceptions on a regular basis. Even with those we know well, it's hard for us to intuit and recall their deepest motivations. This is why it can be revelatory to see your colleague's Birkman report, where their feelings and perspectives can be articulated in an objective, nonjudging way.

DROUGHT AND DISTRESS

Trees bloom where they're planted if their basic needs are met *most of the time.* As it is for our interpersonal stress, biological stress is not immediately seen but is cumulative. During Houston's 2011 severe summer drought, I saw our Memorial Park trees appear to withstand the drought for more than six weeks, but when the temperatures stayed triple-digit and the rain didn't come by the end of July, the park's pine forest stress began to be visible, turning brown and showing their distress. A tree, like us, can survive some degrees of drought or frigid temperatures, provided that their natural needs are generally met over time.

Returning for a moment to my tree analogy, the other tree metaphor that works well for me is this: we identify the kind of tree it is based on what we can see above ground. The visible part (what we term Usual behavior) of the tree tells us if it's an oak or a pine. While the tree changes in appearance as it matures, the biological identity of the tree never changes. This is true for us. We can choose to adapt certain behaviors as we age and experience life, but we don't change (or need to change) the essence of who we were born to be. For every tree, in addition to the above ground part that shows us its type, there is the critical root system (our interpersonal Needs) that nourish and anchor the tree.

Simard's research goes even further to reveal that this underlying part of the tree has its own language and needs: "A forest is much more than what you see."[9] Though mostly unseen, these underlying roots enable the long-term survival of the tree. If drought threatens the trees, as it did for us in Houston, we begin to see signs of distress: leaves turning brown, branches falling. At this point, we can see that the trees are in stress; their unmet needs are visible.

This happens for us as well. We can have one bad day, or one unproductive interaction, and as resilient humans we can cope with this minor setback. However, when this happens too many times, we're unable to maintain our positive Usual behavior, and we begin to show signs of distress. Like the drought-stricken tree, not only can others see this, but we also feel less than our best.

---

9   Suzanne Simard, "How Trees Talk to Each Other," filmed June
      2016 TED Conference, video, 18:19. https://www.ted.com/talks/
      suzanne_simard_how_trees_talk_to_each_other.

BELOW THE SURFACE

What do trees and their root systems have to do with understanding human behavior? In certain ways, we humans are not so different from trees. As healthy, functioning people, we rely on our external style to relate to others. These socialized behaviors we define as positive are the observable parts of us that help us function in the world of work and relationships. Because this behavior is observable, it causes others to draw conclusions about our behavioral styles.

However, like trees with their underlying root systems, there's more to us and to our personalities than what is seen. Like the tree with its aboveground presence and its belowground root system, we function by effectively blending two distinct but intertwined sets of perceptions.

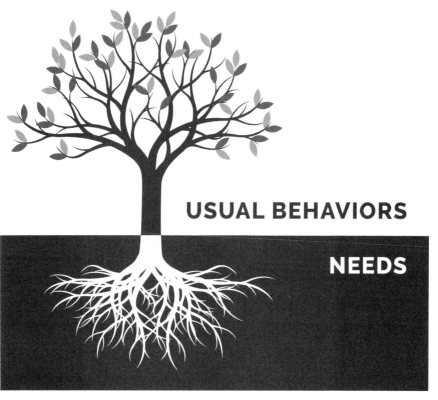

Usual Behaviors and Needs

What we call Usual Behavior is the part of our personality that is acknowledged by us and visible to others. It's our preferred and effective way to relate and connect with others and the way we *usually* show up to interact and get things done day-to-day with people.

However, if we *only* address the observable parts of personality (from the ground up), we're ignoring a significant part: our underlying Needs. Even though the Needs (roots) aren't easily seen, they matter. For us, as socialized humans, these relational roots are the perceptions that recharge us. Our "roots" are the expectations and perceptions Birkman calls our Needs. Needs are fundamental, mostly hardwired, and innate. Unlike our Usual behavior, which we can choose to adapt, Needs tend to change very little over time.

THE BIRKMAN METHOD LOOKS AT FOUR DIMENSIONS:

- **Interests:** As we'll discuss fully in the next chapter, these are the activities that most energize and motivate us. They are usually seen from early childhood and tend to remain consistent throughout our lives.

- **Usual behaviors:** The "aboveground," visible part of our personality. These are our outwardly socialized behaviors and are "usually" positive and productive. It's the approach we've learned works best for us and is the way we prefer to show up on a daily basis.

- **Needs:** Just as the tree is sustained by its roots, humans are sustained by our invisible Needs. When recognized, these interior Needs nurture and empower us, but if they are denied, they can be our greatest liability. Since Needs serve as our own individual root system, we must recognize and understand them. They are vital to our quality of life.

- **Stress behaviors:** Like Usual behaviors, our Stress behaviors are visible. We feel it, others see it. Birkman Stress behaviors are defined as always counterproductive, and even if it looks like progress is being made, it's at great cost to the individual and those around them. Like trees in a drought, when our internal Needs go unmet day after day, we start to experience stress, and we begin to show the less productive sides of our nature.

It is not surprising that most of the time, when asked about their greatest challenge, leaders and teams reply: "It's communication." Why does communication top the list year after year? At Birkman, with our millions of data points, we're in a unique position to answer this question because we can prove that an overwhelming majority of people have underlying motivational Needs that differ from their outward behavior. This is not a conjecture or an opinion, it is a fact derived from our statistical database.

This statistic offers a huge clue about why it's so easy for us to misperceive and so difficult for us to get communication right in every situation. Recalling the platinum rule, if we communicate with others the same way they interact with us, we rarely succeed in meeting their mostly hidden Needs. It's no small wonder communication remains such a challenge. The underlying Needs that work for me—my root system—may be totally opposite from what works best for you. If you think perfect communication is hard to achieve, you're not alone.

When I'm asked to cite only one thing that makes Birkman stand out among assessments, I would have to answer that it's our ability to make the invisible, visible when it comes to perception. This is the fundamental power of what my psychologist father pioneered. He discovered that human relational Needs vary widely between individuals. However, whatever kinds of psychological Needs you and I have, they are all more than okay. None are intrinsically good or bad, better, or worse than others. Similarly, a case can easily be made for how completely acceptable and normal the opposite watering needs of plants are—whether it's the "minimal water, please," orchid or the "I'm very thirsty" hibiscus, both are perfectly okay!

HAVING THIS KNOWLEDGE IS IMPORTANT FOR ANY RELATIONSHIP. IT BECOMES MISSION CRITICAL IF YOU SERVE AS A LEADER.

It is important to remember that our inner Needs cannot be determined (or seen) by observing a person's Usual behaviors—it is one of the main reasons our best attempts at good communicating can fail or fall short. Having this knowledge is important for any relationship. It becomes mission critical if you serve as a leader.

THE EXTROVERT AND HIS INNER POET

Not long ago, I had a Birkman conversation with a high-level senior executive who'd asked to experience the Birkman after I'd presented at a coaching conference. Taking the assessment, he described himself as an action-oriented, decisive, and gregarious person, and indeed he was. Over his lengthy career, he'd successfully presented himself in exactly that extroverted way. Inwardly, he was completely the opposite. His Needs (roots) were those of a deeply reflective introvert. In the first few minutes of our conversation, as I talked him through his results by phone, he interrupted me to say, "This is wrong. I agree with the Usual and with the Interests, but describing me with those particular Needs, no—I have to say you missed me here—they're just flat-out wrong."

As he continued to push back, I let him know we could stop the call and save ourselves the time if he preferred. Instead, he insisted he was curious to hear what else the Birkman revealed, so I soldiered on. A long forty-five minutes later into the conversation, he reluctantly began to admit that his underlying Needs *might be* correct after all. Finally, as we neared the end of our call, he paused for a few moments. Then he sighed … and quietly said, "When I was young, what I really wanted to be was … a poet, but I abandoned that dream. I felt I couldn't disappoint my family by being an English major—it would never be secure enough or pay enough, so I gave it up. I chose to be a business major instead."

He'd spent a lifetime masking his inner strengths as a thoughtful and deeply empathetic introvert. To survive in a world where he perceived it be a professional mandate, he'd worked hard over the years to build and uphold the image of a hard-driving, decisive, extrovert. His inner poet may have been concealed, but it never really died because these were his roots. His love of literature, his appreciation for beautiful language and poetry, were important parts of who he was born to be. His roots were his truth, and they were never going to change.

Before ending our call, I did my best to convince him that his inner poet was nothing to conceal, that it was his strength, not a weakness. I assured him the introvert at his core had helped to make him a successful executive coach, that it was a power he should own, not something to deny. By the time we finished our conversation, he finally acknowledged the value of digging deeper into the internal Needs and Interests that define us. In the last moments of our call, he even expressed a desire to add Birkman to his coaching tool kit. He was tough to convince, but I was hopeful that he would decide, after all, to accept his own valuable truth.

When we examine the dual reality of all our perceptions as both/ and, or as the tree itself *and* its roots, we're able to see a more complete picture of our human behaviors. Our Usual (outward) behavior combines organically with our roots or (internal) Needs, giving us depth and power. We don't want to deny this part of ourselves. In fact, unmet Needs result in chronic stress that will be seen in all our relationships and can negatively impact our health. The word *disease (dis-ease)*—the state of being without ease—frequently begins with interpersonal stress. Living day after day in a forced version of ourselves takes a great deal of energy. Ultimately, it can burn us out.

Just as for the businessman/poet, it's tempting to hide parts of ourselves, especially if society deems certain traits to be *better, stronger,* or more *impressive.* Striving to act/look like a total extrovert if your real power is being an internal introvert can take a toll and deplete us over time. When we're aware of our internal (root) motivators, then we, like my mighty oaks, are far better equipped to withstand the inevitable storms of life.

WHY BIRCHES?

In my final year at Harvard Business School, after my OPM (owner/ president management) class had experienced Birkman as a group, they asked me to select a thank-you gift for my father. The gift committee had located an artist who crafted individual tree sculptures from thin wire and natural stone. Each sculpture was a distinct work of art, with many varieties of trees featured in his catalogue. When I came to the page with birch trees, I thought of my original Bavarian family name: Birkmann is German for "Birch-man." Reading the artist's description, I realized the birches were also a perfect metaphor for us. Birches are distinguished by the fact that no single birch tree can stand alone or survive in isolation. The artist's catalogue read: "Birches can only thrive *in relationship* to at least one or more birches." Their underground root system is a complex, interwoven, and interdependent network. Perfect! It was not only my family name, but it was also the ideal image and metaphor for what the Birkman is meant to do for people.

The birch tree, a gift for my father from my class at Harvard, is displayed in the Birkman International office.

My father always called the Birkman a relational tool, designed from the start for social comprehension. How do I see others in the world? What do I generally expect from other people? Once again, it's never just about me and understanding myself; it's also about how I best relate to you and to all the others in my life. When I can see both, I can do a better job of managing myself. The constant kaleidoscopic shifting of our interpersonal Needs and motivations makes human perceptions both compelling and confounding. No assessment, including ours, is a silver bullet, but it can start a healthy dialogue. Armed with a deeper understanding of your root system (Needs) as well as your branches (Usual Behaviors), it's easier to self-manage and provide essential self-care. Even more importantly, you can avoid defensiveness and discover how to offer others what *they* need.

If trees in a forest can communicate and care for one another through their underlying root systems, then we as evolved human beings can do even more. The highest and best use of Birkman is to use awareness and insights to offer compassionate connection to one another.

TAKEAWAY TIPS

- High-value relationships require a mutual understanding of one another's strengths and needs.

- When our interpersonal Needs go unmet over time, we begin to experience frustrated and unproductive Stress behaviors.

- It's helpful if we communicate our Needs to those who live and work with us.

CHAPTER 6

CONNECTING AT THE ROOTS

The Restorative Power of Motivational Needs

We are all unique ... and so is everybody else!

—Dr. Ellen Langer

I n earlier chapters, we looked at the relationship between our (visible) usual behaviors and our (invisible) motivating Needs. The following real-life stories are examples of the relationship between the two. Often, this Birkman Needs dynamic can make the difference between true connection and fractured relationships. Names have been altered for privacy, but here are a few of my own personal stories that illustrate the impact of these unseen but powerful motivational Needs.

THE COMPLEMENTARY POWER OF TWO

The organizational mandate for departmental pairing usually dictates who is assigned to work together. What we discovered in this story is that, whenever possible, it's just as important to pair colleagues according to their internal Needs as according to their work assignment. Here's how this played out in our own office.

TESSA'S STORY

We hired Tessa, a bright and creative young lady coming straight from college with very high recommendations. On the Birkman, one of her more pronounced Usual Behaviors was a Birkman Component we call Insistence, which for Tessa was exceptionally high. This meant she could—and, in fact, preferred to—bring her own self-driven process to the task at hand. People with high Insistence also believe there's a system and a right, methodical way to do things. In sharp contrast to her Usual behaviors, Tessa's *Need* for Insistence, namely the amount of externally imposed structure she wanted from others, was extremely low.

At the start of her employment with us, she was assigned to the marketing department, which looked to be an ideal place for her creativity to bloom. She officed with Emily, another creative young colleague who happened to also share Tessa's high Usual Insistence trait. Coincidentally, this implied that Emily also *preferred to rely on her own systems and procedures, rather than on someone else's.* Both young women were highly productive and valuable employees, but in this one aspect, it was as though we'd unintentionally paired two positive magnets together.

Over time, this similarity began to be become more and more of a challenge for the two. Ironically, in addition to the "too similar" Usual strengths, these two valuable employees also happened to share the same motivating Needs. In the final analysis, no one was at fault in any way, but this particular workplace pairing had placed them in a situation that, over time, was not proving optimal for either of these talented employees.

Meanwhile, also working in our office was my daughter Amy, VP of Product Innovation. Amy is a spontaneous and superflexible creative as well, but she's at the other end of the spectrum with very *low* amounts of Usual Insistence, the trait Tessa and Emily possessed in abundance. In addition, in contrast to the other two, Amy's *Need for Insistence* was *higher* than her Usual, so she *expected* others to be more process- and plan-oriented than she was. In fact, she greatly appreciated the ability of others to bring process and structure to support her innovative initiatives.

When we paired Tessa with Amy in the Product Innovation department, the new working chemistry was sudden and dramatic. It was obvious we'd put two powerful magnets together. With their *opposite* behavioral strengths and Needs, they very quickly established a partnership that was complementary and productive. Amy's ability to create a big-picture vision was beautifully complemented by Tessa's ability to help structure the necessary details of their common goals.

YOU CAN MINIMIZE FRUSTRATING CLASHES AND BUILD PARTNERSHIPS THAT LEVERAGE DIFFERENCES AND PROMOTE PRODUCTIVITY.

The dynamic between Amy and Tessa also worked well because they shared a solid awareness of each other's strengths and underlying Needs. Without this understanding and respect for each other's contrasting styles, Tessa might have been tempted to question Amy's less orthodox leadership style, while Amy might have felt that a new team member coming in and trying to impose her own structure and plan was undermining her executive authority. There can be many reasons for conflict, but frequently in workplace situations, dissonance between two employees can rest on just such a seemingly small and subtle relational issue. Amy and Tessa's story proves that when you objectively understand the complementary power of two, you can minimize frustrating clashes and build partnerships that leverage differences and promote productivity.

JUSTIN AND LEXI: A STUDY IN CONTRASTING NEEDS

As we know, human personality is complex. This means that within each of us, we can have introverted and extroverted tendencies, even within the same traits and types of behavior. When it comes to perceptions and behaviors, our Usual and our Needs can be totally opposite and may alternate in a dynamic and healthy dance between the two. This may sound confusing, but it's perfectly normal and works well for us most of the time. For an example of how this can play out, let's look at the contrasts in Justin's and Lexi's Social Energy scores.

My friend Justin is an ambitious millennial who works in sales, managing high-level accounts for a large biopharma company. If you met him, you would describe him as an extroverted, high-potential professional who makes a great impression, and clearly, his career is on the rise. His job includes some client travel, and he's quick to tell you he genuinely enjoys meeting new people and visiting new places. However, he'll also confess that long, full days of social interaction with groups of people wears him down. In fact, he often wondered why, as such a very social person with plenty of physical energy, being in long meetings with groups of people so exhausted him. The commissions were high, and Justin knew he was good at sales, but he'd even begun to question his career choice. If this was truly his dream job, why did he feel such a desperate need to escape everybody by the end of the day?

When Justin saw his Birkman, the answer was obvious. He was indeed very social, and this was the highly extroverted Usual (99 percent) part of his behavior. However, for Justin, this very high *Usual* was partnered with a very low Need (2 percent) for spending time alone or with just one or two people. At Birkman, we call this introverted side of Justin his Need for being on his own or "selectively social." If we revisit my tree analogy, Justin's visible "trunk and leaves" showed him to be a classic *extrovert*, and the root system that nourished him showed him to be intensely *introverted*. Justin had outstanding people skills and was excellent with his clients, but to restore his social batteries, he required significant time alone or with just a special friend or two.

Now that Justin knows his Social Energy Needs, he finds it easier to exercise self-care. After long days in group meetings, he's learned it's okay to politely decline social engagements that extend into the evening. He lets his friends and coworkers know what he's learned about getting his internal Needs met. He now reassures them that when he declines invitations, it's about his own self-management and in no way a rejection of them. Justin is also a dedicated husband and the father of three young children. Recognizing his need for some independent time, he rises at four thirty each morning to give himself some quality alone time before the rest of the family is up and going.

By intentionally recharging his Social Energy batteries in these ways, Justin is doing his entire family a favor, and knowing this about himself has boosted his career performance as well. Justin's story is a great example of how understanding underlying Needs, "standing on your own roots," with keener awareness allows you to better self-manage and build stronger, healthier relationships.

Occupying the other end of the Social Energy Needs spectrum is my youngest daughter, Lexi, an interior designer. Since early childhood, she's been a person who thrived on being around people. Whereas Justin required some independent time on his own to recharge, Lexi is a *High Usual with High Needs*. She can recharge after work and on weekends by being *with groups of people*. Unlike Justin, being with people in social situations does not tire her; instead, being with people *energizes* her. In Lexi's perceptual world, she expects others to be similarly social, and she can comfortably interact with other people until she's simply worn out—not socially drained, just physically exhausted. In contrast to Justin, if Lexi spends too much time alone, she finds it more demoralizing than restorative.

Earlier this year, she decided to exit one of the city's leading design firms to start her own company. As a newlywed, she thought it financially prudent to work from home, and for the first six months, this is what she did. She tried hard to tough it out working day after day all by herself, but as we know, Birkman Stress is cumulative. Finally, after months of struggling in isolation, she was invited to share an office with another young designer, and even though the two were working separately on their own projects, just being in the company of another person was enough to boost her social energies. Right away she exclaimed: "I got more done there on the first day than I'd been able to do in an entire week when I had to work at home and all alone."

With their sharply contrasting Social Energy Needs, both Justin and Lexi are completely normal. What is important to note is that while they *appear similar in the ways they show up, they recharge in dra-*

matically different ways. For Justin, being "on" and outgoing demands a great deal of behavioral energy. He perceives that being friendly and outgoing is how he's at his best, and he does this very well *if* he can recharge his Social Energy batteries with some time alone during or at the end of the day. Certainly, like most of us, Justin can push himself when the work or family situation demands, but for the most part, it's important he have some regular and consistent time alone to stay at his best.

In either case, there's absolutely no judgment here regarding Lexi's and Justin's opposite Needs for Social Energy. However, if I were to hire them and want to keep them productive, it's important for me to allow Justin to have some time to work independently and to minimize nonessential group events and meetings. Conversely, for Lexi, I can diminish her productivity, or even demoralize her by separating her too often from the team or asking her to work alone for extended periods, or to work entirely from home.

Another thing to keep in mind when putting two people together: if we put Lexi and Justin together on the same team, they will need to understand that just because they behave similarly on the outside doesn't mean they recharge in the same ways at the end of the day.

If they were assigned to work together without knowing their opposite Needs, Justin would have to work even harder to carve out the down time he needs to recharge and avoid long group meetings, while Lexi might be disappointed if Justin avoids her requests for additional meetings or and might be frustrated or perplexed when he continually seeks ways to socially escape.

When we pay attention to these powerful internal Needs, they give us strength. Acknowledged, they allow us to take better care of ourselves and connect more easily with others. Social Energy is only one of nine Components we measure, but each of the traits we call behavioral Components work together like the organs of the body, and when we're at our best, any and all of them can serve as a competitive advantage for us. However, if we disregard our Needs, then these behaviors can become a liability—not only for us but for those nearby.

* * *

As a newbie leader at Birkman, I was taught a valuable lesson by one of our long-tenured employees. Beverly had deep institutional knowledge of Birkman, so from my first day, I knew she was a valuable resource. Brimming with novice enthusiasm, whenever I had a question or a new idea, I trotted down the hall to share my thoughts with her. What you should know about the two of us is this: on my Birkman, I enjoy being physically active and responsive to varying demands on my attention, thriving on daily variety, and looking for excuses to spend restless energy. Like my daughter Amy, I have low amounts of the Birkman Insistence Component and am much less process- and detail-oriented than Beverly, who is very good at staying focused and on task. You may suspect where this is going ...

For quite a while, Beverly politely tolerated my style, but one day she looked up from her computer to say, "Sharon, I'm happy to speak with you or help you, but it's better to send me an email first. I usually respond quickly, but I need to pay close attention when I'm working so I don't make mistakes."

Of course, Beverly was exactly right. It was important she was willing to remind me of her own Need to stay on task, something we strongly encourage people to do. If I had taken a moment to reflect on Beverly's Needs and expectations, I'd have known that. Instead, I made an all-too-familiar mistake. Forgetting to consider Beverly's working style, I acted only from my own perceptions, oblivious to our contrasting strengths and Needs. My behavior reflected my preferences for variety and quickly shifting tasks, while Beverly's contrasting *strength* was her ability to stay focused and be superattentive to necessary detail. Indeed, this conscientiousness was one of the many reasons she'd been so successful in her various roles at Birkman. Her willingness to share her own Needs was a good wake-up call, reminding me once more how easy it is to forget that my own specific Needs often stand in stark contrast to the motivational Needs of another person. It was all too easy for me to assume Beverly would be fine with my behavior since, after all, it worked for me! This is a risky assumption, however, for me or any of us to make. It's dangerous to assume that what I happened to enjoy coincided with what Beverly preferred, but it made for a memorable lesson.

However well-meaning we are (and I believe most people usually are), when we overlook others' interpersonal Needs, we can cause unintentional conflict. Over time, this can harm relationships and may even erode trust. The good news is that awareness and coaching can help.

These many years later, I'm still grateful for that early lesson. Beverly shared what she needed from me and why it mattered. In the grand scheme, our organization benefits from what each of us brings to the company with our complementary styles and helps to provide the essential diversity we'll discuss toward the end of the book.

What I do know for sure is this: if everyone in our company were just like me, we'd be in serious trouble. Our organizational success benefits from employees who measure all over the behavioral and Interests spectrum. This is the kind of individual diversity that enables us to grow and get better. When we create corporate cultures that value diverse perceptions and behaviors, we improve engagement and retention. Our team members know that what enables our success is their wide variety of perceptual styles as well as their skills and talent.

As Beverly did for me, it helps to share with colleagues what we need from them. Done with care, it lets others know you're using your own self-awareness (along with your others-awareness) with the goal of being a better work or life partner. The behavioral differences we have are relationship critical, and when others kindly point them out, as Beverly did, they do us a huge favor. Although people and their Needs will differ in all kinds of ways, it is the willingness to communicate and understand them that promotes healthier, more productive relationships.

If I am placed in a leadership or a supervisory role, it might be tempting to expect the employees to adapt to my natural leanings and style. However, a true leader's role is to recognize and enable the diverse styles of every employee and to build an appreciation for this diversity in a culture and environment that sets everyone up for success. It never works if I hire in my own image or force all employees to conform to the mold of my own personality and expectations.

FIRE AND WATER

I'm not proud of this fact, but I've noticed that I find it remarkably easy to describe others' behaviors with negative words if I am frustrated with them and to use positive terms when I'm pleased with them. The reality is that I am mostly addressing the very same trait and describing the very same behavioral style. For example, when I'm happy with them, they are "conscientious, thorough, and attentive to detail," and when I'm frustrated with them, they are "stubborn, rigid, and inflexible." Or for my colleagues who are very direct and matter-of-fact communicators, on good days, I see them as "welcome and candid straight shooters," and on difficult days, they are "offensive and blunt." In both situations, I'm referencing the same personality traits.

In each case, context matters along with two more factors that make a difference: first, me and my own perceptual filters in that moment, and second, whether the other person is applying their own behavioral traits in a productive (positive) way or in a frustrated (negative) and stressed-out way. In either case, it helps the situation if I know myself and am aware of *their* hardwired tendencies. In and of itself, just being self-aware may not remove the "ouch" factor, but it can diffuse, or at least help to minimize, some of my anger and defensiveness. I can make a choice to "take it less personally" in my working relationships when I have objective insights into the contrasting perceptual styles that at the end of the day are so necessary in our organization.

FLIP SIDES OF THE SAME COIN

How can it be that the very qualities we call our strengths are also our weaknesses? When and how does my strength become my liability? Think fire and water. Both fire and water are essential to our survival. Both are life giving when under control, and deadly and destructive when out of control. This applies to each of the personality traits and perceptions we address through the Birkman. Every behavioral trait we describe with the Birkman Components has the potential to be a genuine strength, and at times even a superpower for us if applied in the right way and in the right context.

Our strengths become our problems when they are exaggerated, overused, or misdirected, like too much water that turns into a flood, or the gas flame that cooks my dinner, goes out of control, and burns down my home. Where and when does negative behavior rear its head? There are too many causes of stress to count, but from a social psychology standpoint, one cause of nonproductive stress in relationships happens when we fail to recognize our own or the other person's Needs and expectations. For another way to think of our Usual behaviors, you could compare these outward behaviors to tools we use to get work done or to build relationships. In some situations, our own set of tools work well to fit the job at hand, but in other situations they do not. We've got to match the tool to the job at hand—wrenches work for bolts, not screws. Like the good craftsman who knows exactly which tool to use, awareness is key. Just as every problem is not a nail, every relational Need is not the same, even though the person with a hammer may see (perceive) every problem as a nail.

Even when I have all the right tools for the task at hand, it's still possible to misuse them. Carpenters know there's a limit to how much I can bang on the nail—too much force with the hammer and I break it—leaving me with an even bigger problem than I had before.

Since we each have only so many tools in our individual toolboxes, it's important to know when we're missing the proper tool. These are the times we especially need connection, when we rely on the importance of what others bring and when we reach out to *those who do* possess the right tools for the job.

Leadership coach and our VP of training, Dan Perryman, described his own strengths and blind spots in a "Why Birkman?" blog he wrote while he was still working as a learning and organizational development expert for the Walmart corporation:

> *The primary reason I feel so strongly about The Birkman Method is that it personally changed my life and the results I*

had been getting in my career. I was a mid-level leader who was struggling with who I was and frustrated with the complexity of corporate relationships. When I received the results of my Birkman report, they exposed the lies I had been telling myself. My strengths were clear, and I could own those. My biases were also clear, and I realized that the story I had created about my struggles was just that: a story. When I faced those perceptions and opened my mind to what else could be true, things changed for me. I'm still learning every day, but it was the kick-start my Birkman gave me that got it started.

A Birkman assessment can serve as a productive step forward in developing self-awareness, but true self-awareness is learning when our Usual behaviors are serving us—and when they are not. I would hope that for all of us, we can feel confident enough in our own strengths to come out from behind the persona of any masks we feel we ought to wear. I would hope for all of us to dare to be vulnerable enough to pierce through the biases as Dan did, enabling us to lead ourselves and to relate to others more effectively.

I'd claim some remorse or at least some compunction,
but I just can't help it. My form is my function.

—David Rakoff, "Speak Now or Forever Hold Your Peace"

USING THE EMOTIONAL INTELLIGENCE FRAMEWORK WITH BIRKMAN CONCEPTS

For our Birkman trainees and coaches, Dan incorporated a helpful framework to consider using Daniel Goleman's Emotional Intelligence (EQ) framework, which can be summarized into four key activities: Self-Awareness, Social Awareness, Self-Control, and Social Skills. The chart on the next page overlays some relevant Birkman principles onto Goleman's four quadrants.

REGULATION

OTHERS — SELF

RECOGNITION

SOCIAL SKILLS

RELATIONSHIP MANAGEMENT

- Proficiency in managing relationships and building social networks
- Ability to flex your behavior to meet the needs of others
- Expressing your own expectations in a socially acceptable way

SELF-CONTROL

ADAPTABILITY, RESILIENCE

- Controlling disruptive impulses and attitudes
- Constructive use of nervous tension and energy
- Suspending judgment about those who are different from you
- Learning to think before acting on emotion alone

SOCIAL AWARENESS

READING EMOTIONAL STATES

- Attention to the emotional states of other people
- Realization that others may be wired differently than you are and may react differently to the same situation
- Awareness of social norms and standards of behavior

SELF AWARENESS

EMOTIONAL / RATIONAL BIAS

- Tracking your own moods throughout the day
- Awareness of your emotional load in different circumstances
- Understanding which activities recharge your batteries and which drain the positive energy from you

Because we're measuring each person's individual perceptions, all the Birkman dimensions discussed in this book falls into the Self-Awareness quadrant. Birkman describes the perceptions that show us how we logically and emotionally process the world around us.

Self-awareness and **social awareness** are all about knowing how accurately I'm perceiving my own behaviors and the behaviors of others. Am I able to see and recognize those moments when others are experiencing life differently? Am I paying attention to social norms—and how they change depending on the group and the circumstances? Self-awareness is knowing what tools I have in my toolbox, and social awareness is recognizing and appreciating the tools of others. The more we understand, the better we can connect.

Self-control is the internal action to stop a negative behavior or attitude that's not getting us the result we're wanting—knowing when my hammer isn't the right tool and reaching for a wrench instead. Exercising self-control is much easier if you're aware of who *you are* as well as what *others are* and what they need from you.

When we're aware of ourselves and others, we can channel that awareness into a positive outcome in our relationships, thereby exhibiting influential **social skills**. As I look back, all four of these were important in my early learning experience with Beverly, and thankfully, my mistake didn't run her off. Beverly is still a valuable asset who is still contributing. That memorable early lesson has made for a more productive working relationship for me, and hopefully for Beverly as well.

TAKEAWAY TIPS

- It's easy to feel disconnected if we lack an understanding of the other person's strengths and needs, the reality of *their* perceptions.

- Sometimes our strengths can be misdirected or overused, either by using the wrong behavior for a situation or by overdoing the right one.

- It's my responsibility to share my own Needs. When I know the other person's perspective or perceptions, it's easier for me to be less defensive. I'm less likely to hold a grudge or feel personally attacked.

CHAPTER 7

INTERESTS: THE THIRD DIMENSION OF NEEDS

Ideally, work should be for the grown-up what play is for the child.

—Roger Birkman

M y mother's childhood dream was to play the violin, but as she grew up in the 1920s as a child of the Depression, there was no money for the musical training she so desperately desired. On more than one occasion, she told me she'd skip lunch to pay for her violin lessons, but instead of playing in a symphony orchestra, her family determined she should train for a practical clerical job—a job she hated. Her musical ambitions and any hopes for college were crushed by her family's more pressing need for a paycheck.

Fortunately, she also dreamed of making the world a better and more understanding place, so when she met my father, her career dream began to evolve into *their* career dream. Despite the strong interest they shared in social psychology and the slowly growing success of the small start-up business she helped him build, there were times throughout her life that my mother never seemed completely satisfied with her own achievements. Battling some periods of depression throughout her life, she always seemed to carry the wounds and disappointment of being denied a chance to study music or earn a college degree. Perhaps this was one reason she was especially passionate about wanting people to honor their own interests, often reminding us of the toll an unfulfilled life can take on the human spirit. Now, as a mom myself, I know she enjoyed seeing her own children pursue their interests and dreams so easily, using the opportunities she helped make possible.

Classical music, an interest she passed to me, was a cornerstone of her life. From the time I experienced my first opera at age five—*Madame Butterfly*—I told my parents I wanted a career in music. As I look back, I appreciate that my laser focus on the arts was never questioned by my parents; in fact our mutual love of classical music was something that created a strong connection between us, something we enjoyed together.

When I was sixteen, Dad let me take the Birkman questionnaire for the first time, and as expected, my interests in music and literature topped the charts. Unlike my mother, I *was* given the opportunity to study music. As a young teen, I practiced for hours a day to be a serious concert pianist but found far greater joy (and connection!) in the more sociable world of music theater during my college years. Despite my love of music, sitting alone at the piano for hours each day had been socially isolating for me. Throughout my teen years, I was a shy introvert who felt like an odd duck with my passion for "serious music," and I was lonely. By my junior year of high school, I was fortunate to attend the Interlochen Arts Academy in Michigan, and there I found connection to other kids who were like-minded. By the time I got to university, in addition to meeting my Social Energy Needs, the world of musical theater and opera now connected me to others who truly shared my interests. In the words of Joseph Campbell, I'd discovered "my bliss"!

For me, musical theater/opera was a place where gifted people combined multiple arts into one big collaborative team project and worked together to bring a production to life. I'd finally found my place of belonging, and by graduate school, I'd determined that performing in and directing musical theater was my chosen path. And indeed, this career choice fulfilled me for many years. Unlike my mother, I got to do what brought me joy. She and Dad had always supported and encouraged my music studies, and this is a great gift for parents to offer their children. Without question, our core interests (as careers or hobbies) are powerful lifetime magnets that energize us and enhance our well-being.

Not only in our jobs, but also when it comes to personal time, Birkman Interests reveal the kind of activities that make us feel happier and healthier. These ten general Interest categories have survived over time and have been translated across countries, making Birkman the only assessment that integrates job families and careers with perceptions and behaviors. Over the years, our top Interests continue to define what keeps us engaged and energized—both at work and at play.

BLAKE'S STORY:
VITAMINS FOR THE SOUL

When Rachel, one of our Birkman employees, married Blake, he already had a successful corporate career. But despite the security his job provided, Rachel often saw Blake come home from work looking drained and dissatisfied. She decided to review Blake's Birkman report with him and when she looked at his Birkman Interests, she saw that his Outdoor scores (95 percent) were off-the-charts high. In fact, this implied that his Outdoor score was more than a casual need. It was a mandate for Blake. Outdoor Interests that are that high indicate someone who, in a perfect world, would want to spend their professional life *working outdoors.*

Unfortunately for Blake, nothing about his office career afforded this. As a Birkman-savvy wife, Rachel understood the link between her husband's interests being absent in his day job and why he was becoming more and more demoralized and disengaged. Initially, they tried to meet his outdoor needs by making time to camp, hike, or garden on weekends—something they both enjoyed. This helped, but for someone whose Interest level was as sky-high as Blake's, it was not enough. What Blake needed was a career that gave him daily opportunities to be outside.

Rachel and Blake discussed the practical realities of a career shift and agreed he could try a new job. He was hired by the local nature conservancy and now works outdoors every day. Even in the brutal heat of Houston summers, Blake comes home happier. Rachel reports the spike in his energy was dramatic, saying, "When I come home from work now, I come home to a different husband. He may be hot and tired, but he's in better spirits. It's a *good* tired now." They may have to budget more carefully for a while, but Rachel's smile says the change was worth it. The benefits to their marriage and shared happiness outweigh their material sacrifice.

For many people, as with my mother, there are times when a job change is impossible or unrealistic. If this is the case, it's even more critical to pay attention to the top several interests. When we talk to people who feel, for whatever reason, they can't leave their jobs, we encourage them to pay special attention to their top Interests and find ways to include them in personal time. When you create time for your Interests, even in small doses, your spirits rise and your morale improves. This is because, the highest three or four Birkman Interests are another form of individual "Needs." Interests serve as important motivators—both in and out of the workplace.

VITAMINS FOR YOUR SOUL: INTERESTS ARE MORE THAN JUST "INTERESTING"

Over the years, we've heard many stories about the ways Interests impact overall physical and emotional health. Soon after I began working full time inside Birkman, a Boeing organizational development executive shared his story about coaching an SVP through her Birkman Report. She worked a demanding office job, and like Blake, she had very high Outdoor interests. She confided the guilt she felt about trying to rush home from work each day to spend "too much time" in her garden. Her OD coach reassured her, "When you pay attention to your top interests, you're doing vital self-care. You are making yourself a happier, better leader for all the people in your division. When you find time for being outdoors, you are more productive in your day job. Given your high Outdoor needs, gardening is vitamins for your soul."

These Birkman Interests, such an important part of who we are, appear to be born into us, and they develop early. When we pay attention to them, they contribute in significant ways to mental, physical, and emotional well-being. If you're able to include at least one or more of your top Interests in your daily job, you're more engaged at work and less stressed at home. Blake's need to work outdoors was innate, clearly hardwired into his DNA. He'd landed a practical indoor job and could do the work, but at what cost? When he was able to shift to a career that featured his top Interest, his well-being and relationships improved. This is the kind of happy ending we often see when an important Interest Need is met.

LIFE IS TOO BRIEF FOR YOU OR ANYONE YOU LOVE TO BE MISERABLE AT WORK.

Life is too brief for you or anyone you love to be miserable at work. Admittedly, financial security is an issue, and life circumstances make this much easier for some than for others, but if you work in a job that doesn't include at least *one* of your top three or four interests, please *give yourself permission to include them in your personal time*. There's no denying that our interests serve as energy rechargers and "vitamins for your soul." As the garden-loving corporate executive was told, she was not wasting her time. Neither are you. Even if you're not getting paid for it, you're investing in yourself and practicing worthwhile self-care. Do it for you. Not only will *you* be happier, your friends and family will be happier to be around you!

PUTTING IT ALL TOGETHER

We can create healthy connections by showing an interest in others' Interests, taking a moment to be curious about what fascinates them—even when it's not one of your top interests. When we meet someone who's interested in something we know nothing about or may not even understand, it can break down barriers and build healthier connections. Connection deepens when you show you care about something they care about. When your own Interests are fulfilled, you become more of your best self, and when you're at your best, you bring out the best in others.

TAKEAWAY TIPS

- Interests are powerful magnets for us; they are vitamins for our souls.

- Research strongly indicates we're born with specific interests that motivate us.

- Our top Birkman Interests recharge us and restore our energy. Our lowest Interests can drain our energy and, if possible, are best delegated.

- For peak emotional health, top performance, and engagement in our careers, we must find ways to include our top Interests in life, whether at work or in our personal time.

CHAPTER 8

CONNECTION, CONVERSATION, AND COLLABORATION

*The privilege of a lifetime is being who you are. When you realize
that you and the other are in fact, one, it's a big realization.
Survival is the second law of life. The first is that we are all one.*

—Joseph Campbell

Several years ago, my husband and I were staying in New York
City while he was singing performances at the Metropolitan
Opera. When I introduced myself at a group event, a lady heard my
name and asked, "Are you Birkman from that personality test?" This
can be a loaded question, as many people are fearful of any kind of
"personality test" or might want to take issue with the results.

As I nodded yes, she continued, "I work for the Junior League
here in Manhattan, and we use your assessment on a regular basis.
I want to tell you about a woman in our office who made my life
miserable. I couldn't stand her. But when we did the Birkman with
our team, for the first time, I understood her communication style,

her Needs, and how *she perceived me*. After that, I even began to recognize the value she brought to our team. I used to be convinced she had it in for me, that she was just *trying* to annoy me, but after we did the Birkman, I realized it never was about me at all. By being who she was and bringing her different perspectives, our team was actually stronger in ways I never appreciated until that day." Smiling, she added, "We get along pretty well now; in fact … we've even become *friends!*"

Happily, this is not an unusual story for us to hear but is always a welcome reminder that being able to objectively see others through a Birkman lens can make a profound difference in relationships. When we see how our own perceptions compare or contrast with the way others perceive us, it's easier to defuse much of the defensiveness and judgment that prevents communication and harms relationships. It's my conviction that, regardless of the strengths and talents we each have, we're all meant to be born "incomplete" and for a very good reason. It is our interdependence and need for one another that brings us together, the relational glue that unites us. Objective social science, used well, can tear down some of the walls of misperceptions that frequently get in the way of connection and collaboration.

Medical experts tell us that learning to walk is one of the hardest *physical* challenges a baby will ever overcome. Social scientists report that our ability to communicate with others, which starts to evolve as soon as we acquire language, is one of the most difficult *psychological* and *social* feats we humans ever face. We learn to *talk* early in our lives, but every day, we continue to learn how to *communicate*.

British anthropologist Robin Dunbar discovered that the strongest predictor of a species' brain size is determined by the size of its social group.[10] The conclusion was that having a larger brain is what allows us to communicate, to become social creatures who can connect with one another. Dunbar's research makes clear that *the human brain is made for and enhanced by personal connection* and collaboration.

In his book *Social: Why Our Brains Are Wired to Connect*, psychologist and neuroscientist Matthew Lieberman addresses *how* we're made for connection. His studies concluded that when the brain is not involved in a task, it falls into a state called the "default network."[3] And this configuration is almost identical to the social thinking we use to make sense of ourselves and others. He writes, "The default network directs us to think about other people's minds—their thoughts, feelings, and goals."[11] Whenever our brains have a moment, we default into a social reflex. "Evolution has made a bet," said Lieberman in an interview, "that the best thing for our brain to do in any spare moment is to get ready for what comes next in *social* terms."[12]

HOW SOCIAL PSYCHOLOGY BRINGS IT ALL TOGETHER

At Birkman, we're in the business of social psychology, which is defined as the study of how our thoughts, feelings, and behaviors are influenced by the actual, imagined, or implied presence of *others*. Currently, we've established user bases across six continents, enabling

---

10   R. I. M. Dunbar and S. Shultz, "Evolution in the Social Brain," *Science 317*, no. 5843 (2007): 1344–1347. doi:10.1126/science.1145463. PMID 17823343.

11   Matthew Lieberman, *Social: Why Our Brains Are Wired to Connect.* New York: Crown Publishers, 2013.

12   Emily Esfahani Smith, "Social Connection Makes a Better Brain," *The Atlantic,* Oct. 29, 2013, https://www.theatlantic.com/health/archive/2013/10/social-connection-makes-a-better-brain/280934/.

us to collect social data from all over the world. The Birkman is available in twenty-three languages, with more to come. With the data from millions of assessments, we have an exclusive perspective on the underlying perceptions, behaviors, and interests of our worldwide culture. If we look at different people from around the world, we see incredible surface variety. Even within our own country, the regional differences between the states make our world a more exciting place. It is important to note, however, that these differences are not what I'm talking about with our human perceptions and interpersonal differences.

Differences we see from country to country fall into the category of *learned behaviors*. The *outward* distinctions—how we look, our mannerisms, and traditions have evolved over time from various cultures and communities. It's easy to assume that where you were born and raised would influence the perceptions you have of yourself and the world around you. However, when it comes to the interests and traits we measure on the Birkman, we continue to see responses from across the globe that human expectations and perceptual trends hold across cultures. At the heart of our humanity, we humans (regardless of generations, gender, or country) are more similar than we'd imagined, and our social science is affirming this to be true.

Throughout the writing of this book, it's no secret that my country's political climate has been, and still is, volatile and divisive. It's also no coincidence that political strategies over recent years have hinged on dangerously reinforcing people's political ideology by creating a digital environment that one's own perception is the most popular, that the way I see things is the only "right" or "true" way to think. Social media lacks the restraints of responsible journalism and continues to perpetuate and support whatever side it's seeking to promote. If we're limited to the messaging that only affirms existing agendas and partisan beliefs, we're cut off from the diverse perspectives that enrich us as a democracy. This divisive political phenomenon also speaks to another kind of perceptual power and the danger of avoiding real conversations with those who disagree is that it prevents us from connecting with those who are most different. As we'll talk about in the final chapter, a diversity of perception is what truly strengthens teams, families, and societies.

If we have no peace, it is because we have
forgotten that we belong to each other.

—Mother Teresa

For another insight into the power of connection, Sally Kohn, in her book *The Opposite of Hate*, asserts that the biggest factor in fighting hate is personal connection. Kohn's book makes a potent case to prove that *connection is the opposite of hate*. Like my NYC friend who told me about her annoying coworker, once there was a real conversation about their differing perceptions, it was harder to dislike her colleague. When we have an empathetic encounter with another, a chance to truly communicate, it's much easier to connect and understand. This is because, as has been proven many times over, it's very difficult for us to hate people close up.

CONSCIOUS LISTENING

Becoming a good listener is another powerful way for us to better connect with others. A British expert in "conscious listening," Julian Treasure, also a self-proclaimed advocate for better listening, puts forward a memorable formula to help us improve our listening skills. He offers the four-letter acronym RASA, explaining that it in Sanskrit, *rasa* means "juice" or the essence. In Treasure's helpful mnemonic, the *R* stands for Receive, the *A* is Appreciate, the *S* is

Summarize, and finally the *A* is for Ask. Ask more questions and keep on listening.

Several years ago, we made an internal change in our own terminology. For many years, the industry term we'd used for giving a person information on their Birkman report was called "a Birkman feedback." When Dan Perryman arrived, I enthusiastically welcomed his suggestion that we change this term to a "Birkman conversation." Whenever we conduct a Birkman Certification course, on the final day of class, our new trainees head off to do their first official Birkman "conversations" with a partner from their class. We advise these almost-certified consultants to try to listen as much or more than they talk. As they review the information, the role of the Birkman coach is not to "read the tea leaves" or simply define terms, but instead to help the recipient put the data into context, to help the person connect the dots by asking how the scores might play out for them in their life. Doing this well requires some heavy-duty listening and the more we listen, the more we begin to understand. The more we understand, the better we connect.

THE MORE WE UNDERSTAND, THE BETTER WE CONNECT.

While working on this book, I was inspired by the TED talk of Drew Philp, a young journalist who used his entire savings to buy himself a trashed-out home in a run-down neighborhood of Detroit. Before Drew could even think about living in it, he had to haul away more than ten thousand pounds of trash from the long-abandoned structure. As he labored to do this all by himself, his neighbors began to take notice. They watched as, day after day, he worked alone to haul away the piles of garbage. They saw him struggling to clear the debris and clean out the mountains of trash. After a while, gradually and one by one, the neighbors began to offer to help Drew. As more decided to join in, more and more were willing to help, and over time, the entire neighborhood had rallied to help Drew rebuild his home. Drew describes how this brought all of them together into a state of "radical neighborliness" that collapsed barriers and united them as friends.[13] His story speaks to how people can connect and transcend barriers when they have a shared purpose. Drew's moving story shows that "radical neighborliness" not only heals alienation and segregation, it also brought connection and joy.

WHY AM I HERE?

At a recent conference called "The Power of We," one of the speakers was an attorney from California named Bob Goff. Having just read his book *Everybody Always*, I'd signed up to go because I wanted to see him speak and was curious how the evening's theme might align with this book's theme. However, on the day of the event, heading there straight from a long day at work with no time for a break, I arrived tired and hungry. Added to this, my social batteries had been drained by a full day of group meetings, so I deliberately chose a seat near the back, comfortably distant from everyone else and where I might make a quick getaway if desired.

The session started as the evening's facilitator welcomed us and immediately asked everyone (oh no!) to get up and move to the center to sit closer together. Reluctantly, I got up to move, thinking, *Okay but please ... just don't ask us to talk to each other too much tonight.*

As soon as we all resettled, the emcee announced, as I'd feared, that our assignment was to have a follow-up conversation with a

---

13   Drew Philp, "My $500 House in Detroit—and the Neighbors
     Who Helped Me Rebuild It," *TED Talk*, NPR, September
     28, 2018, https://www.npr.org/2018/09/28/652305575/
     drew-philp-how-can-radical-neighborliness-help-struggling-communities.

person sitting nearby after each speaker's topic. Given my less-than-ideal mood, my initial perception of my opinionated talking partner was not particularly charitable. On top of everything else, it happened to be the night before the US midterm elections, and political electricity was hard to avoid. To me, this man seemed arrogant, even pompous, but as I was *still working* on my book about the importance of connecting, I made a little extra effort to keep my negative thoughts from preventing a worthwhile conversation.

The evening wore on. More speakers, more assigned conversations with the same assigned partner until finally, it was almost 9:00 p.m., the time we were scheduled to end. At 8:56 p.m., relieved, I started to pack up my belongings. Preparing to make my dash to the door, I heard the moderator announce the final assignment of the evening … and I was stuck. One last conversation and no hope for a graceful exit.

For the concluding assignment of the evening, we were to ask each other, "*What do you fear?*" Eager to wrap things up, I asked the self-assured man—who I knew, by this time, held strong and opposing political opinions—this final question. He grew quiet, and I braced myself for another tedious exchange. He hesitated for a few moments … and then softly, he whispered: "*Bullying … I fear bullying.*"

What? Really? This was *his* answer? This was the answer from a man I'd perceived as overbearing and imposing? The same man who'd projected such a confident demeanor throughout the evening? Of all people, *he fears bullying*?

He then began to tear up, and his voice trembled as he spoke: "Just over a year ago, I lost my son. He was a victim of bullying."

He told me how proud he was that his severely autistic son, a bright college freshman, had worked hard and had managed to make it to university to live on his own in a dorm. His son was doing fine with his grades but felt socially isolated and so humiliated by the bullying that, tragically, he'd committed suicide. He went on to say, "My son was a victim of cyberbullying. He killed himself to escape the online social media taunts."

In that moment of heartbreaking connection, I forgot my self-focused hunger and fatigue. Instead, I felt I suddenly knew why I had been there all evening. Yet another opportunity to be reminded of my own flawed and limited perceptions. In an instant this man's bearing shifted from bravado to fragility. What triggered such a shift?

It was asking the question. Simply *asking* him what he feared had encouraged his vulnerability and allowed him to share in a deeper way. With that one simple question, his dedication as a loving father connected with the parent in me. I knew I couldn't begin to comprehend the staggering grief of a child's suicide or the burden he bore as a shattered parent trying to deal with this incomprehensible loss. But in that moment of profound connection, all else faded into insignificance. Whatever our earlier differences might have been, in that moment of connection, we found it easy to agree on the need for a world with more compassion, more kindness, and greater understanding. He shared with me his battle to go on living, to find any meaning still left in his life. He said he was working hard just to keep breathing in a world without his son. He said that was why he'd shown up that evening. It was part of his effort to rejoin life for the sake of his wife and the rest of his family.

For me, the lesson of the evening was to be reminded once again of this truth: at the level of deep human connection, our external differences become trivial. They really don't matter at all. As Bob Goff, our speaker of the night, had said:

"We don't grow where we're informed. We grow where we're accepted."[14]

THE COMPLEXITIES OF CONNECTION

For human relationships to flourish, we must keep on seeking to listen without judgment and be willing to engage in real conversations. When a conversation becomes a dialogue that allows us to connect, we can always find ways to collaborate. Yes, I know it's always easy enough to say this and to know this, but why is it so difficult for us to *do* this?

If we're social beings who require safe, human connection to survive, why is daily communication such an ongoing challenge in our relationships, at work, and at home? Countless times I've heard business owners make a remark that sounds something like this: "I'm fine when it comes to running the operational side of my business, it's just the *people* side that always makes it so hard."

Here's one reason why. As discussed in chapter 4, when we observe outward behavior, we draw conclusions about the other person from *what we see*. Since our data shows the vast majority of people have a behavioral style that is different from the way they prefer to be treated, it's very easy for us to misperceive. As discussed in earlier chapters, for accurate social comprehension, we must also recognize that what people need to feel motivated may be completely different from their outward demeanor and the external behaviors we observe or perceive to be true. Once we understand this about the person, it becomes much easier to collaborate ... and to forgive.

---

14   Bob Goff, "The Power of We," interview, *Q Commons,* October 25, 2018.

TEAM POWER

In crucial things, unity. In important things,
diversity. In all things, generosity.

—**George H. W. Bush (on teamwork)**

Since nothing gets done to completion by a single individual, the topic of team building always remains front and center in the world of business. Over my career, I've seen how the greatest successes in our firm have relied on at least two people who consistently spark and support one another. In their book *The Power of 2*, Gale Muller and Rodd Wagner cite the elements that make or break a partnership: complementary strengths, a common mission, fairness, trust, acceptance, forgiveness, communication, and unselfishness.[15]

If you follow the trail of what's been successful in virtually every endeavor, it tracks back to *at least two people* who complemented each other's gifts and worked in tandem to achieve what neither could do on their own. Whatever the goal, whatever the project, personal or professional, every successful person I've met or observed always has a "second," a special colleague who enabled their success. In another example of productive synchrony, Simon Sinek's *Start with Why* identifies two types of people: the WHY-types are the visionaries and the HOW-types make it happen. As Sinek writes: "Those who know *why* need those who know *how*."[16]

Dr. Matt Gosney is vice president for organizational health at UC Health in Denver, Colorado, and is also an outstanding Birkman expert. Frequently, in HR and OD circles, we tend to focus most of

---

15   Rodd Wagner and Gale Muller, *Power of 2: How to Make the Most of Your Partnerships at Work and at Life*. New York: Gallup Press, 2009.

16   Simon Sinek, *Start with Why: How Great Leaders Inspire Everyone to Take Action*. New York: Penguin Press, 2009, p. 140.

our attention on the complexities of communication within a team, but Matt emphasizes another important aspect: "The communication lapses are not so much *within* each team and individual department, but often the breakdowns occur at the seams *between* the departments." In other words, it's not just that employee A doesn't get along with employee B; it's also that B's team doesn't communicate well with A's team. Somehow, there's been a failure *to connect* the teams. These dynamics can be tricky, especially as companies grow. The larger the company, the more employees must work to permeate the seams between departments. Today's world of digital and virtual teams can add yet another layer of complexity to issues of human connection and communication.

Where office spaces are concerned, the debate continues regarding the benefits of open versus private offices, but the importance of communication remains a constant. There are many ways to tackle the challenges of working better together, and I work every day with an instrument that can be hugely helpful, but I believe the natural complexity of human perceptions and personality is one reason it is, and will continue to be, such a dynamic and ongoing challenge.

CONNECTING WITH YOU HELPS CONNECT WITH ME

As mentioned earlier, social science has proven that connecting with other people, even in the most basic ways, *literally* makes people happier and healthier—especially when we feel we're helping each other. In many cases, it can be as simple as a tiny gesture.

As an example of just how small it can be, best-selling author Jen Sincero writes of boarding a plane for her first solo trip to India. She recalls how excited she was to go but also how terrified. When she got to her assigned seat, she describes how a beautiful Indian woman sitting beside her turned, smiled, and offered her an M&M's candy. Sincero writes, "And that's when it really sank in. You are not alone, you ding dong. You are surrounded by people."[17] In that moment of accepting another's simple kindness, she says she suddenly knew everything would be okay. So hardwired are we to respond to small acts of kindness, of human connection, that something as simple as a smile, a kind word, or a piece of candy was enough to calm her fear. That subtle shift in perception was a little miracle for Jen, a reminder that when we simply reach out, or open ourselves up to connection, none of us is truly alone.

CONNECTION SHRINKS THE REPTILE BRAIN

Krista Tippett's *On Being* interview with neurosurgeon James Doty speaks to a way medical science also demonstrates our drive for connection. Dr. Doty explains that one way we're differentiated from animals is by having offspring who rely on us for most of the first two decades of life. As a result of this, Doty says, "There had to be these very, very powerful pathways that bonded us with our offspring and these neuropathways result in us feeling good when we connect."[18] He goes on to assert that connection isn't just something we seek in order to achieve more effective conversation and collaboration, *it's actually good for your health*. He explained that with today's neuroscience technology, a surgeon can literally see how *fear ignites the amygdala* part of the brain, that most primitive (reptilian) part of

17 Sincero, Jen. *You Are a Badass: How to Stop Doubting Your Greatness and Start Living an Awesome Life.* Philadelphia: Running Press, 2013.

18 James Doty, "The Magic Shop of the Brain," interview by Krista Tippett, *On Being,* February 11, 2016, https://onbeing.org/programs/james-doty-the-magic-shop-of-the-brain/.

our brain that controls our fight or flight instinct. He witnessed that when people get a feeling of psychological safety and connection, he could *see the amygdala get smaller*, literally shrinking in size. This means that, as fear subsides and we experience supportive human connection, the amygdala literally gets smaller in size. Where there is connection and a feeling of trust and psychological safety, our fight or flight reaction calms down.

The testimony of a neurosurgeon affirms that connection with others makes us not only happier, but quite literally, healthier. In his memoir *Into the Magic Shop,* Doty writes, "Our journey isn't meant to be an inward journey alone, but an outward journey of connections as well. When we go inward, and our heart is open, we will connect with the heart, and the heart will compel us to go outward and connect with others."[19]

* * *

As I learned from my discussion partner that evening at the "We" conference, human connection is always about the conversation. When we line up on different sides, when we get our shields out or wear masks, it's impossible to connect. There's no space for conversation, and nothing hurts more than refusing to have a compassionate conversation, because it's vulnerable and authentic dialogue that builds trust and promotes psychological safety. When it comes to company cultures, this is what can measurably increase engagement and ROI. Empa-

NOTHING HURTS MORE THAN REFUSING TO HAVE A COMPASSIONATE CONVERSATION.

---

19   James Doty, *Into the Magic Shop: A Neurosurgeon's Quest to Discover the Mysteries of the Brain and the Secrets of the Heart.* New York: Penguin Random House, 2016, p. 231.

thetic conversations empower teams and enable collaboration, and this means healthy human connection is a mandate, not an option, for healthy and strong company cultures.

TAKEAWAY TIPS

- It's easy to feel disconnected when we lack an understanding of the other person's strengths and needs, the reality of their perceptions.

- However difficult it may be, we must come together for meaningful connection, and sometimes the tiniest gesture of kindness can be powerful.

- Connecting with others in a positive way makes us healthier and happier. Supportive human connection can literally shrink the amygdala, which is the fear-based "flight or fight" part of our brain.

CHAPTER 9

ESSENTIAL DIVERSITY

We connect through what makes us the same. We
contribute with what makes us different.

—Torri Olanski

T hough it's tempting for leaders to hire in their own image, successful leaders are those who gather the most diverse strengths
and perspectives to populate their teams. Probably most of us are
drawn to those who think as we do, but this particular temptation is
especially dangerous in a leadership role because it's so easy to like the
people who share our interests, mirror our style, and think like we
do. After a Birkman session in Boston, a West Coast business owner
bounded over to my dinner table to exclaim, "Sharon, after learning
about Birkman with our group today, I know what I've been doing
wrong since I started my technology company. I've hired a team of
fifteen engineers, and this afternoon I realized why we're not more
successful—they're all me! All fifteen of them are just like me!" While
it may be comfortable for birds of a feather to flock together, we
know for sure that every company requires the varying perspectives of
diverse work and personal styles. In the right context, every organiza-

tion succeeds best when they welcome a wide variety of perceptual styles and when they can boast a healthy balance of what I like to call essential diversity.

There is much discussion in the corporate world about diversity and inclusion. While I am grateful for this, I believe diversity is more than race, gender, generations, or socioeconomics. What I call *essential diversity* includes our wide variety of unique interests, mindsets, perspectives, and social perceptions—in other words, the genetic DNA of all our inborn traits. And no team, village, or corporation can survive, let alone flourish, without this kind of diversity.

IN OUR OWN IMAGE: THE CULTURE ALWAYS MIRRORS THE LEADER

Author Susan Cain explores communication complexities in her 2012 groundbreaking book *Quiet*. Seeking to more fully understand her own introversion, she probes the research and studies the upside of being born an introvert "in a world that can't stop talking."[20] Although she'd reached a career high, she discloses how unfulfilled she was, working to play the role of an extroverted Wall Street attorney. With a vote of confidence from the man who would become her husband, she left the legal world and turned to her first love, being a writer. Susan Cain embraced the gift of her true introversion and dared to trade a lucrative position for the literary career she'd always wanted.

Staying home to write her book, Cain describes the tension she was feeling between the need to interact with people versus her need to sequester herself to write and reflect. After working to carefully set up her "ideal office" at home, she realized she was stuck and dis-

20   Susan Cain, *Quiet: The Power of Introverts in a World that Can't Stop Talking.* New York: Broadway Paperbacks, 2013.

covered she couldn't write. It was altogether too quiet. Even as an introvert, she felt too isolated, too cut off from everyone. So she left her ideal home office, gathered up her laptop and wrote most of her book at her favorite, bustling neighborhood coffee shop. She found that the mere presence of other people coming and going in a social setting created the hum of the environment she needed to help her focus and write. She found her best writer's energy in the livelier environment.

Cain writes that "the way forward … is to actively seek out symbiotic introvert-extrovert relationships, in which leadership and other tasks are divided according to people's natural strengths and temperaments. Studies show the most effective teams are composed of a healthy mix of introverts and extroverts and so are leadership structures." What we see day to day, going far beyond introversion or extroversion, is paying attention to the diverse social Needs, Interests, and individual styles that ultimately create the most vibrant and enduring cultures.

As discussed in earlier chapters, there are many ways we're very similar to people living on all sides of the globe. At the same time, there are many things that differentiate us from those who share our homes, offices and neighborhoods. Where there are individual differences, I call them essential since they exist because we need them. What we can see in our database is that there are thousands and thousands of different combinations and intensi-

WHAT WE CAN SEE IN OUR DATABASE IS THAT THERE ARE THOUSANDS AND THOUSANDS OF DIFFERENT COMBINATIONS AND INTENSITIES RELATING TO THE WAYS PEOPLE PERCEIVE SELF AND OTHERS.

ties relating to the ways people perceive self and others. Let's make sure we never define diversity as only what we can be seen on the outside. When we consider the infinite array of perceptions people have, we realize diversity goes well beyond what is visible to our eyes. How do we leverage this diversity I'm calling essential? Listen. Stay open to hearing diverse viewpoints and perspectives. Every conversation is a way for me to begin a positive dialogue about you and your perceptions. Ideally, my best role is to understand and appreciate who you are and the value you can offer.

We know from the Birkman scoring that there's enormous diversity in the ways people answer the same questions. This is a very good thing, as diversity is what makes teams, organizations, neighborhoods, and communities successful, and all organizations, regardless of their size or purpose, need this kind of diversity. In fact, studies show that organizations that are more diverse come up with better ideas, are able to solve more complex problems, and ultimately will generate more profits. Yet while all these things are very attractive, diverse organizations may require more effort to manage. Like the business owner at the beginning of this chapter who hired fifteen engineers just like himself, it's very easy to surround ourselves with others who perceive the world as we do. While this certainly feels comfortable in the short term, it's at the expense of long-term success.

While I've been banging the drum loudly for diversity and the value of contrasting perceptions and styles, it's important to remember we still share a profound common humanity. Nature mandates variety, so here we are in all our inexhaustible, infinite details, no two of us born exactly alike. In a world of incredibly diverse humanity, we share our *need for connection* to others, and the *need to be accepted by another human*. In the moments of our lives when we feel most validated and connected to those who matter to us, like my mighty row of old oaks, we become the best versions of ourselves, strongly rooted in who we were born to be.

My father was a lifelong fan of the French writer and aviator, Antoine de Saint-Exupéry, often saying his book *Wind, Sand and Stars* sparked his desire to be a pilot. When I was seventeen, I read Saint-Exupéry's *Le Petit Prince* for the first time, and to this day, I regard it as one of the wisest books on relationships ever written.

As the Little Prince grows weary from roaming the planets, he encounters a very wise Fox. The Fox tells the Prince that for them to become friends, the Prince will first have "to tame" him. For this taming, the Fox tells the Prince he will need to arrive at the same time every day, each day sitting just a bit closer so that over time, trust can build and their friendship will grow. The Fox says, "My existence is rather boring and monotonous. I hunt chickens and men hunt me." He then goes on to say, "If you are willing to tame me, it will be as if the sun has come to shine on my life."

The Prince tells the Fox he'd left his own planet because he was frustrated with his Rose, and the Prince suspects she may have already "tamed" him, but he hesitates, telling the Fox: "I'm busy—I have so little time, so many things to discover and understand." The Fox replies, "It's the time you have wasted on your Rose that makes your Rose unique. One only understands the things one has tamed. We have no more time to understand anything."

Human connection demands *our presence* in one form or another. It's hard to have quality relationships with colleagues, friends, or family "in a hurry" or from too great a psychological or geographical distance. Not every friendship, job, or relationship will endure or is destined to last for a lifetime, but there's little space to argue that "the time we have wasted" on our authentic and deepest relationships is anything other than one of the best investments we will ever make.

What is essential is invisible to the eye. It is only
with the heart that one can see clearly.

—Antoine de Saint-Exupéry

As we learn from the Fox, the time spent listening or simply "being there" for one another may not feel productive up front, but it's essential for building healthy and enduring relationships. The time we spend with our teams connecting and appreciating one another's differences might be the first thing we cut from our busy schedules, yet it's arguably one of the most important things we can do if successful organizations are our long-term goal.

In the final analysis, essential diversity is the distinctive mind-set and perceptual/personality blend that's born into each of us. When and where we feel genuinely connected and accepted by others, there is trust. We're liberated to bring our special talents and perspectives to the people around us—at home, at work, and at play. When we value essential diversity, the world is a more welcoming place for our children and their children. Diverse though we are, we all bleed the same, and we all require connection with others who, though they may wound at times, still forgive, laugh, and cry with us. For, in the words of Ram Dass, "At the end of the day, we are all just walking one another home."

There's no denying we're complicated, perfectly imperfect, individually distinct yet interconnected beings who strive to get along as creatures of contact. Whether we call it the need for social comprehension, compassionate understanding, or simple acceptance of self and others, in the end it all comes down to what the pastor's son turned pilot turned social psychologist said in a video interview at the age of eighty-eight:

If we can find our purpose, that love and acceptance of who we are, and we're able to see that potential in everybody we meet, that would be a legacy I would dream about … and that's what it's all about really—love.

—Dr. Roger Birkman,
from his "Life Stories Alive" conversation,
taped on August 17, 2007, with Michael O'Krent

AUTHOR'S NOTE

M ike Harrell gave me permission to share this deeply personal email he wrote to my daughter Amy on April 20, 2019. In it, he affirms the value of the Birkman itself but also emphasizes how, when our social science was combined with compassionate human connection, it had the power to transform his life and career.

Amy,

Thank you for hosting the Perception Prison webinar. I agree with you and Birkman that our personality is an incomplete illusion of who we are and that how we perceive the world around us influences our behavior. I also agree that if we don't understand our mindset or worldview and how it's different from others, then we are in a prison. However, I think Birkman not only removes the bars of the prison but actually releases us from the prison.

Let me share a little of my own Birkman journey. I spent twenty-eight years of my career with several multinational companies and thought I'd taken just about every assessment that was on the market at the time (new ones keep emerging). I had been assessed to death, and with one company, I had an all-day battery of assessments to make sure I was the right one for the job. Throw on top of that numerous "team building" experiences and I should be very self-aware and an awesome leader, right? Not really.

We were living in Tampa at the time and my brother kept telling me about this assessment called Birkman, of which I hadn't heard, and that I needed to take it. You can imagine my response was not positive and I resisted for several years. Then finally, at a very low point in my career, I decided to take it because I trusted him and his mentor and, didn't have anything to lose. You know my brother Mark and may have known his coach, Dave Stoddard. I didn't know Dave well at the time, but I liked how he was challenging Mark and the impact he was having on him, so I took the assessment.

That was 2003 and because Dave was in Atlanta and I was in Tampa I never got a personal conversation, or an official interpretation. I printed out a copy of the report he emailed and took it with me on a trip to south Florida, where I had an important meeting, thinking I'd read it in my hotel room that evening. I remember pulling up to the meeting location, taking a quick scan of the report and throwing it against the car door thinking it was just like all the others I'd taken and I didn't like what I was reading. That was my prison for the next year as my career challenges worsened. Fast forward to the fall of 2004 when I was passing through Atlanta to see family and I was able to schedule some time with Dave to finally do the interpretation. We spent about two hours together and the bars came down and the doors opened! Using the reports, Dave looked into my soul and helped me clarify who I really was as a person. The Birkman actually *freed* me to live out of who I am and how I'm wired.

At the end of 2004 I chose to resign from the company I had been working for, and moved to Chattanooga to get closer to aging parents who were in ill health. Not having a job waiting on the other end, I had the unique opportunity of reinventing myself. I decided to start a business advisory practice where I would help leaders navigate through their challenges and bring vision clarity to their business and their own personal lives. As I got involved in the lives of these leaders, I realized I needed a tool to help them understand their own perceptions and their impact on their teams and other people. I became Birkman certified in 2006 and Birkman is now the foundation of my practice and a requirement for every client. What I love about my new career is I get to help clients uncover their issues and perceptions and learn to live freely out of who they are.

So your grandfather had an indelible impact not just on my life, but my wife's, our kids (we gave them and their spouses the Birkman for their wedding presents), and my clients! I'm very grateful for Mark's insistence for me to take the assessment and the ongoing, almost weekly, dialogue we have about how to make the Birkman more impactful in the workplace.

So my mindset (worldview) is that Birkman set me free to live out of how I'm made. Amy, I have the privilege of proclaiming liberty to the captive and freedom to the prisoners and Birkman is the objective, non-threatening tool, that helps open that door. Thank you for carrying the baton of your grandfather's legacy to the next generation!

Mike

ACKNOWLEDGMENTS

It won't surprise you, dear reader, to know that there are many who deserve my gratitude. Harking back to the year I first heard David Rakoff say we're *creatures of contact*, I remain grateful to NYC literary agent, Giles Anderson. As the catalyst for my first book, Giles gave me the courage to tackle a second.

A lion's share of credit goes to Diana Sheley, my right-arm at work and a powerhouse Birkman colleague. Exactly two years ago, Diana partnered with me for a visit to Charleston to meet with Advantage Media Group/ForbesBooks where, on the spot, we committed to this book. Diana, who never seemed to doubt I could do this, serves as a singular force inside Birkman for positive future growth and has been a source of "can-do" encouragement throughout this writing journey.

Huge thanks also to writer/editor Summer Flynn who was assigned by Advantage Media to get me going and that she absolutely did. I was not an easy client for Summer, but she was always patient and consistently supportive, and she pulled me out of my ideas quagmire every time I got stuck, which I did on multiple occasions. Without Summer's enthusiasm for our topic and her guidance in talking me through the bones of the book as she helped me build a working outline, I'd still be treading water in a sea of random "good" ideas.

I'm grateful as well for my gifted daughter, Amy Shepley, who along with her talented innovation colleagues, Torri Olanski and JP

Dowling, helped in the final months as a strong conceptual resource and a helpful sounding board for thoughtful ideas and subject-matter debate.

Special thanks must go to Richard, my sweet and supportive husband of thirty-two years, who possesses many astounding talents but will likely not be reading this book. With his low Birkman Literary Interests, Richard has limited interest in reading books, including mine, but I totally appreciate his patience and understanding over these many months. More times than I care to admit, I missed or abbreviated family events with the panicked cry: "I have to work on my book!"

I also owe an enormous debt of gratitude to the wise, talented, and supremely generous artist and business owner, Linda Limb. She is my covenant friend and neighbor who walks with me every morning at 6 a.m. and has been my confidante, my spiritual go-to, and my "no-matter-what" ally and cheerleader since the day we first met to discuss a design initiative ten years ago.

A special nod to my assistant, Clarissa Rackley, who calmly rescued me each time I needed technical help, which is to say, frequently.

And finally, I'm indebted to the Birkman consultants and employees who've taught me so much over the years. Every day, I continue to learn from you and discover new insights. Together, all of you are the creatures I'm grateful to have contact with. I love you all.